THAI

VISUAL DICTIONARY

T0364478

Published by Collins
An imprint of HarperCollins Publishers
Westerhill Road
Bishopbriggs
Glasgow G64 2QT

First Edition 2021

HarperCollins *Publishers*
Macken House, 39/40 Mayor Street Upper,
Dublin 1, D01 C9W8, Ireland

10 9 8 7 6 5 4

© HarperCollins Publishers 2021

ISBN 978-0-00-839969-6

Collins® is a registered trademark of
HarperCollins Publishers Limited

Typeset by Jouve, India

Printed in India

Acknowledgements

We would like to thank those authors and
publishers who kindly gave permission for
copyright material to be used in the Collins
Corpus. We would also like to thank Times
Newspapers Ltd for providing valuable data.

A catalogue record for this book is available
from the British Library

If you would like to comment on any aspect
of this book, please contact us at the given
address or online.
E-mail dictionaries@harpercollins.co.uk
 www.facebook.com/collinsdictionary
 @collinsdict

MANAGING EDITOR
Maree Airlie

FOR THE PUBLISHER
Gerry Breslin
Kerry Ferguson
Gina Macleod
Kevin Robbins
Robin Scrimgeour

CONTRIBUTORS
Janit Feangfu, PhD
Jacob Marchewicz

TECHNICAL SUPPORT
Claire Dimeo

MIX
Paper | Supporting
responsible forestry
FSC™ C007454

This book contains FSC™ certified paper and other controlled
sources to ensure responsible forest management.

For more information visit: www.harpercollins.co.uk/green

CONTENTS

Whether you're on holiday or staying for a slightly longer period of time, your **Collins Visual Dictionary** is designed to help you find exactly what you need, when you need it. With over a thousand clear and helpful images, you can quickly locate the vocabulary you are looking for.

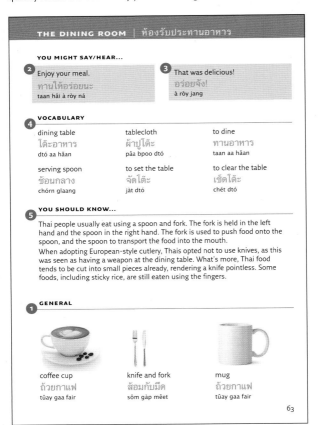

THE DINING ROOM | ห้องรับประทานอาหาร

YOU MIGHT SAY/HEAR...

2 Enjoy your meal.
ทานให้อร่อยนะ
taan hâi à ròy ná

3 That was delicious!
อร่อยจัง!
à ròy jang

4 **VOCABULARY**

dining table	tablecloth	to dine
โต๊ะอาหาร	ผ้าปูโต๊ะ	ทานอาหาร
dtó aa hăan	pâa bpoo dtó	taan aa hăan
serving spoon	to set the table	to clear the table
ช้อนกลาง	จัดโต๊ะ	เช็ดโต๊ะ
chórn glaang	jàt dtó	chét dtó

5 **YOU SHOULD KNOW...**

Thai people usually eat using a spoon and fork. The fork is held in the left hand and the spoon in the right hand. The fork is used to push food onto the spoon, and the spoon to transport the food into the mouth.

When adopting European-style cutlery, Thais opted not to use knives, as this was seen as having a weapon at the dining table. What's more, Thai food tends to be cut into small pieces already, rendering a knife pointless. Some foods, including sticky rice, are still eaten using the fingers.

1 **GENERAL**

coffee cup	knife and fork	mug
ถ้วยกาแฟ	ส้อมกับมีด	ถ้วยกาแฟ
tûay gaa fair	sôm gàp mêet	tûay gaa fair

63

The Visual Dictionary includes:

- 10 **chapters** arranged thematically, so that you can easily find what you need to suit the situation
- **1** **images** – illustrating essential items
- **2** **YOU MIGHT SAY...** – common phrases that you might want to use
- **3** **YOU MIGHT HEAR...** – common phrases that you might come across
- **4** **VOCABULARY** – common words that you might need
- **5** **YOU SHOULD KNOW...** – tips about local customs or etiquette
- an **index** to find all images quickly and easily
- essential **phrases** and **numbers** listed on the flaps for quick reference

USING YOUR COLLINS VISUAL DICTIONARY

The points set out below will help to make sure that your **Collins Visual Dictionary** gives you as much help as possible when using Thai:

1) **How to express politeness**

   When speaking Thai it is often necessary to add small words called particles to the end of your sentences to convey politeness. Men add the word "kráp" and women add the word "kâ". Polite Thai speech is peppered with these particles, but not always at the end of every utterance. It is advisable to use them as much as possible until you get the feel for them. In some of the example sentences in this book they have been included already. For example, a man saying "thank you" would say "kòrp kun kráp" and a woman saying "hello" would say "sà wàt dee kâ". Note that the particle used by women changes to a high tone when it is added to a question, so a woman saying "sorry?" would say "à rai ná ká?".

2) **Personal pronouns**

   There are a large number of different personal pronouns in Thai. The polite first person pronouns (I/me) differ for men and women; men say "pōm" and women say "chán" or the more formal "dì chán". The word "káo" can be used as the third person pronoun for both men and women (he and she), and is sometimes used to refer to more than one person (they). The polite second person pronoun (you) is "kun". This can also be added before someone's name as an honorific prefix.

3) **Classifiers**

   Classifiers are an important feature of Thai and are often mandatory when using a noun with a numeral or when referring to a specific noun. For example, "one student" is "nák rian nèung kon". Here, "nák rian" is the noun meaning "student" but the classifier for people (kon) must be added after the number when specifying the number of students.

There are many different classifiers in Thai, used for different types of objects. A useful general classifier is "an", which can be used to count or pinpoint just about any small object for which you don't know the correct classifier. For example, "an née tâo rài kráp/ká" (how much is this one?).

4) **Tones**

Thai is a tonal language, meaning that each word is pronounced with a certain pitch. Changing the tone will change the meaning of the word. Thai has five tones, and since it also makes the distinction between long and short vowels, there is effectively a long and short version of each tone. You can listen to the free audio resource to get acquainted with the long and short sounds, many of which have been transcribed in this book using double vowels (i.e. "aa" would be a longer sound than "a"). The rules for figuring out the tones in Thai script are complicated, but the pronunciation guide under every entry in this book marks the tones above the vowels in each syllable, as summarised in the following table:

TONE NAME	SIGN	PITCH LEVEL	EXAMPLE	MEANING
mid	no sign added	mid level	ไมค์ mai	mic
low	` (above the letter)	low falling	ใหม่ mài	new
falling	^ (above the letter)	high falling	ไม่ mâi	not
high	´ (above the letter)	high rising	ไม้ máai	wood
rising	ˇ (above the letter)	low falling-rising	ไหม mǎi	silk

FREE AUDIO

Whether you're going to be visiting Thailand, or even staying there for a while, you'll want to be able to chat with people and get to know them better. Being able to communicate effectively with acquaintances, friends, family, and colleagues is key to becoming more confident in Thai in a variety of everyday situations.

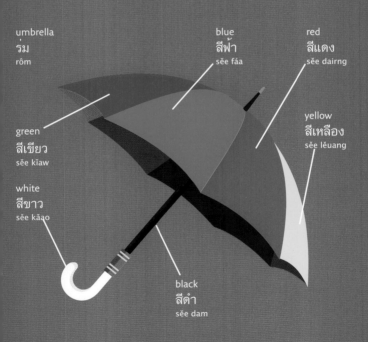

umbrella
ร่ม
rôm

blue
สีฟ้า
sĕe fáa

red
สีแดง
sĕe dairng

green
สีเขียว
sĕe kĭaw

yellow
สีเหลือง
sĕe lĕuang

white
สีขาว
sĕe kăao

black
สีดำ
sĕe dam

Hello.	Good afternoon.	See you tomorrow.
สวัสดี ครับ/ค่ะ	สวัสดี ครับ/ค่ะ	เจอกันพรุ่งนี้
sà wàt dee kráp/kâ	sà wàt dee kráp/kâ	jer gan prûng née

Hi!	Good night.	Bye!
สวัสดี ครับ/ค่ะ	ราตรีสวัสดิ์	ลาก่อน
sà wàt dee kráp/kâ	raa dtree sà wàt	laa gòrn

Good morning.	See you soon.	Good luck!
อรุณสวัสดิ์	แล้วเจอกัน	โชคดี
à run sà wàt	láew jer gan	chôhk dee

YOU SHOULD KNOW...

The most common Thai greeting is "sà wàt dee" (nearly always followed by "kráp" or "kâ" when said by a man or woman respectively). It is equivalent to "hello" in English but it is also used to say "goodbye" when speaking formally or on the telephone. For a more casual goodbye you can say "láew jer gan".

Yes.	Thank you.	I'm sorry.
ครับ/ค่ะ	ขอบคุณ ครับ/ค่ะ	ผม/ฉัน ขอโทษ
kráp/kâ	kòrp kun kráp/kâ	pŏm/chán kŏr tôht

No.	No, thanks.	OK!
ไม่ ครับ/ค่ะ	ไม่ครับ/ค่ะ ขอบคุณ	โอเค
mâi kráp/kâ	mâi kráp/kâ, kòrp kun	oh kay

I don't know.	Excuse me.	You're welcome.
ผม/ฉัน ไม่รู้	ขอโทษ ครับ/ค่ะ	ด้วยความยินดี
pŏm/chán mâi róo	kŏr tôht kráp/kâ	dûay kwaam yin dee

Yes, please.	Sorry?	I don't understand.
ครับ/ค่ะ ขอบคุณ	อะไรนะ	ผม/ฉัน ไม่เข้าใจ
kráp/kâ, kòrp kun	à rai ná	pŏm/chán mâi kâo jai

YOU SHOULD KNOW...

In Thai, different words are used to mean "please" depending on the context. For instance, when asking someone to do something for you, you can make the sentence more polite by adding the words "dûay" or "nòy", followed by "kráp" or "kâ".

How old are you?
คุณอายุเท่าไหร่
.kun aa yú tâo rài

I'm ... years old.
ผม/ฉัน อายุ ... ปี
pŏm/chán aa yú ... bpee

I was born in...
ผม/ฉัน เกิดปี...
pŏm/chán gèrt bpee...

Where do you live?
คุณพักอยู่ที่ไหน
kun pák yòo têe năi

Where are you from?
คุณมาจากประเทศ
อะไร
kun maa jàak bprà tâyt
à rai

I'm from...
ผม/ฉัน มาจาก...
pŏm/chán maa jàak...

I live in...
ผม/ฉัน อยู่ที่...
pŏm/chán yòo têe...

I'm...
ผม/ฉัน เป็น...
pŏm/chán bpen

British
คนอังกฤษ
kon ang grìt

Scottish
คนสกอตแลนด์
kon sà gòt lairn

English
คนอังกฤษ
kon ang grìt

Irish
คนไอร์แลนด์
kon ai lairn

Welsh
คนเวลส์
kon wayw

Are you married?
คุณแต่งงานรึยัง
kun dtèng ngaan réu yang

I'm married.
ผม/ฉัน แต่งงานแล้ว
pŏm/chán dtèng ngaan
láew

I have a partner.
ผม/ฉัน มีแฟนแล้ว
pŏm/chán mee fairn láew

I'm single.
ผม/ฉัน เป็นโสด
pŏm/chán bpen sòht

I'm divorced.
ผม/ฉัน หย่าแล้ว
pŏm/chán yàa láew

I'm widowed.
เป็นม่าย
bpen mâai

Do you have any
children?
คุณมีลูกไหม
kun mee lôok mái

I have ... children.
ผม/ฉัน มีลูก ... คน
pŏm/chán mee lôok
... kon

I don't have any
children.
ผม/ฉัน ไม่มีลูก
pŏm/chán mâi mee lôok

YOU SHOULD KNOW...

It is quite normal for young people in Thailand to ask one another's age, and is an important part of knowing how to address each other. However, caution is advised when talking to anyone slightly older as they may find being asked about their age uncomfortable.

This is my...
นี่คือ ... ของ ผม/ฉัน
nêe keuu ... kŏrng pŏm/
chán

These are my...
นี่คือ ... ของ ผม/ฉัน
nêe keuu ... kŏrng pŏm/
chán

husband
สามี
săa mee

wife
ภรรยา
pan rá yaa

boyfriend
แฟน
fairn

girlfriend
แฟน
fairn

partner
แฟน
fairn

fiancé/fiancée
คู่หมั้น
kôo mân

son
ลูกชาย
lôok chaai

daughter
ลูกสาว
lôok săao

parents
พ่อแม่
pôr mâir

mother
แม่
mâir

father
พ่อ
pôr

brother (older)
พี่ชาย
pêe chaai

brother (younger)
น้องชาย
nórng chaai

sister (older)
พี่สาว
pêe săao

sister (younger)
น้องสาว
nórng săao

grandfather (mother's
father)
ตา
dtaa

grandfather (father's
father)
ปู่
bpòo

grandmother (father's
mother)
ย่า
yâa

grandmother (mother's
mother)
ยาย
yaai

granddaughter
หลานสาว
lăan săao

grandson
หลานชาย
lăan chaai

mother-in-law
แม่สามี/แม่ภรรยา
mâir săa mee/mâir pan
rá yaa

father-in-law
พ่อสามี/พ่อภรรยา
pôr săa mee/pôr pan rá
yaa

daughter-in-law
ลูกสะใภ้
lôok sà pái

son-in-law
ลูกเขย
lôok kŏey

stepdaughter
ลูกเลี้ยงผู้หญิง
lôok líang pôo yĭng

extended family
ญาติพี่น้อง
yâat pêe nórng

brother-in-law
พี่เขย/น้องเขย
pêe kŏey/nórng kŏey

uncle
ลุง/อา/น้า
lung/aa/náa

friend
เพื่อน
pêuan

sister-in-law
พี่สะใภ้/น้องสะใภ้
pêe sà pái/nórng sà pái

aunt
ป้า/อา/น้า
bpâa/aa/náa

baby
เด็กทารก
dèk taa rók

stepmother
แม่เลี้ยง
mâir líang

nephew
หลานชาย
lăan chaai

child
เด็ก
dèk

stepfather
พ่อเลี้ยง
pôr líang

niece
หลานสาว
lăan săao

teenager
วัยรุ่น
wai rûn

stepson
ลูกเลี้ยงผู้ชาย
lôok líang pôo chaai

cousin
ลูกพี่ลูกน้อง
lôok pêe lôok nórng

YOU SHOULD KNOW...

You may have noticed that some of the words for relatives change depending on which side of the family they are. For example, maternal grandfather is "dtaa" and paternal grandfather is "bpòo". Siblings are divided into older siblings (pêe) and younger siblings (nórng). In Thai culture, many of these words are used affectionately between people who are not actually related. Besides the affection, there is also an element of age hierarchy and respect for elders involved.

How are you?
คุณเป็นยังไงบ้าง
kun bpen yang ngai
bâang

How's it going?
เป็นยังไง
bpen yang ngai

Very well, thanks, and you?
สบายดี ขอบคุณ
แล้วคุณล่ะ
sà baai dee, kòrp kun,
láew kun là

Great!
เยี่ยมเลย
yîam loey

So-so.
เฉยๆ
chŏey chŏey

I'm fine.
ผม/ฉัน สบายดี
pŏm/chán sà baai dee

I'm tired.
ผม/ฉัน เหนื่อย
pŏm/chán nèuay

I'm hungry/thirsty.
ผม/ฉัน หิวข้าว/หิวน้ำ
pŏm/chán hĭw kâao/hĭw
náam

I'm full.
ผม/ฉัน อิ่มแล้ว
pŏm/chán ìm láew

I'm cold/warm.
ผม/ฉัน หนาว/อุ่น
pŏm/chán năao/ùn

happy
มีความสุข
mee kwaam sùk

excited
ตื่นเต้น
dtèuun dtên

surprised
แปลกใจ
bplàirk jai

annoyed
รำคาญ
ram kaan

sad
เสียใจ
sĭa jai

worried
กังวล
gang won

afraid
กลัว
glua

bored
เบื่อ
bèua

I feel...
ผม/ฉัน รู้สึก...
pŏm/chán róo sèuk...

well
สบายดี
sà baai dee

unwell
ไม่ค่อยสบาย
mâi kôy sà baai

better
ดีขึ้น
dee kêun

worse
แย่ลง
yâir long

YOU SHOULD KNOW...

Thai people address each other differently depending on their age difference. For instance, if you are slightly older than them they may add the word "pêe" before your name. It literally means "older sibling" but can be used to address anyone a little older than the speaker.

Where do you work?
คุณทำงานที่ไหน
kun tam ngaan têe nǎi

What do you do?
คุณทำงานอะไร
kun tam ngaan à rai

What's your occupation?
คุณทำงานอะไร
kun tam ngaan à rai

Do you work/study?
คุณทำงาน/เรียน ใช่ไหม
kun tam ngaan/rian châi mái

I'm self-employed.
ผม/ฉัน ทำงานส่วนตัว
pǒm/chán tam ngaan sùan dtua

I'm unemployed.
ผม/ฉัน ไม่มีงานทำ
pǒm/chán mâi mee ngaan tam

I'm at university.
ผม/ฉัน เรียนมหาวิทยาลัย
pǒm/chán rian má hǎa wít tá yaa lai

I'm retired.
ผม/ฉัน เกษียณแล้ว
pǒm/chán gà sǐan láew

I'm travelling.
ผม/ฉัน เดินทางท่องเที่ยว
pǒm/chán dern taang tông tîaw

I work from home.
ผม/ฉัน ทำงานที่บ้าน
pǒm/chán tam ngaan têe bâan

I work part-/full-time.
ผม/ฉัน ทำงานพิเศษ/ประจำ
pǒm/chán tam ngaan pí sàyt/bprajam

I'm a/an...
ผม/ฉัน เป็น...
pǒm/chán bpen...

builder
ช่างก่อสร้าง
châng gòr sâang

chef
พ่อครัว/แม่ครัว
pôr krua/mâir krua

civil servant
ข้าราชการ
kâa râat chá garn

cleaner
คนทำความสะอาด
kon tam kwaam sà àat

dentist
ทันตแพทย์/หมอฟัน
tan dtà pâirt/mǒ fan

doctor
แพทย์/หมอ
pâirt/mǒr

driver
คนขับรถ
kon kàp rót

electrician
ช่างไฟ
châng fai

engineer
วิศวกร
wít sà wá gorn

farmer
เกษตรกร
gà sàyt dtrà gorn

firefighter
นักดับเพลิง
nák dàp plerng

fisherman
ชาวประมง
chaao bprà mong

IT worker
พนักงานไอที
pá nák ngaan ai tee

joiner ช่างไม้ châng máai	salesperson พนักงานขาย pá nák ngaan kǎai	company บริษัท bor rí sàt
journalist นักข่าว nák kàao	scientist นักวิทยาศาสตร์ nák wít tá yaa sàat	factory โรงงาน rohng ngaan
lawyer ทนาย tá naai	soldier ทหาร tá hǎan	government รัฐบาล rát tà baan
mechanic ช่างยนต์ châng yon	teacher ครู kroo	hospital โรงพยาบาล rohng pá yaa baan
nurse พยาบาล pá yaa baan	vet สัตวแพทย์ sàt dtà wà pâirt	hotel โรงแรม rohng rairm
office worker พนักงานบริษัท pá nák ngaan bor rí sàt	waiter พนักงานเสิร์ฟ pá nák ngaan sèrp	office สำนักงาน sǎm nák ngaan
plumber ช่างประปา châng bprà bpaa	waitress พนักงานเสิร์ฟ pá nák ngaan sèrp	restaurant ร้านอาหาร ráan aa hǎan
police officer ตำรวจ dtam rùat	I work at/in... ผม/ฉัน ทำงานที่... pǒm/chán tam ngaan têe...	school โรงเรียน rohng rian
sailor กะลาสี gà laa sěe	business ธุรกิจ tú rá gìt	shop ร้านค้า ráan káa

morning
เช้า
cháao

afternoon
บ่าย
bàai

evening
เย็น
yen

night
กลางคืน
glaang keuun

midday
เที่ยงวัน
tîang wan

midnight
เที่ยงคืน
tîang keuun

What time is it?
ตอนนี้กี่โมง
dtorn née gèe mohng

It's nine o'clock.
เก้าโมง
gâao mohng

It's quarter past nine.
เก้าโมง สิบห้านาที
gâao mohng sìp hâa naa tee

It's half past nine.
เก้าโมงครึ่ง
gâao mohng krêung

It's quarter to ten.
อีกสิบห้านาทีสิบโมง
èek sìp hâa naa tee sìp mohng

It's 10 a.m.
สิบโมงเช้า
sìp mohng cháao

It's 5 p.m.
ห้าโมงเย็น
hâa mohng yen

It's 17:30.
ห้าโมงครึ่ง
hâa mohng krêung

When...?
... เมื่อไหร่
mêua rài

... in 60 seconds.
... ในอีก 60 วินาที
nai èek hòk sìp wí naa tee

... in two minutes.
... ในอีก 2 นาที
nai èek sŏrng naa tee

... in an hour.
... ในอีกหนึ่งชั่วโมง
nai èek nèung chûa mohng

... in quarter of an hour.
... ในอีกสิบห้านาที
nai èek sìp hâa naa tee

... in half an hour.
... ในอีกครึ่งชั่วโมง
nai èek krêung chûa mohng

early
เช้าตรู่
cháao dtròo

late
ดึก
dèuk

soon
เร็วๆ นี้
rew rew née

later
หลังจากนี้
lăng jàak née

now
ตอนนี้
dtorn née

Monday
วันจันทร์
wan jan

Wednesday
วันพุธ
wan pút

Friday
วันศุกร์
wan sùk

Sunday
วันอาทิตย์
wan aa tít

Tuesday
วันอังคาร
wan ang kaan

Thursday
วันพฤหัส
wan pá réu hàt

Saturday
วันเสาร์
wan săo

January
มกราคม
má gà raa kom

April
เมษายน
may săa yon

July
กรกฎาคม
gà rá gà daa kom

October
ตุลาคม
dtù laa kom

February
กุมภาพันธ์
gum paa pan

May
พฤษภาคม
préut sà paa kom

August
สิงหาคม
sĭng hăa kom

November
พฤศจิกายน
préut sà jì gaa yon

March
มีนาคม
mee naa kom

June
มิถุนายน
mí tù naa yon

September
กันยายน
gan yaa yon

December
ธันวาคม
tan waa kom

day
วัน
wan

month
เดือน
deuan

weekly
รายสัปดาห์
raai sàp daa

weekend
สุดสัปดาห์
sùt sàp daa

year
ปี
bpee

fortnightly
รายสองอาทิตย์
raai sŏrng aa tít

week
อาทิตย์/สัปดาห์
aa tít/sàp daa

decade
ทศวรรษ
tót sà wát

monthly
รายเดือน
raai deuan

fortnight
สองอาทิตย์
sŏrng aa tít

daily
รายวัน
raai wan

yearly
รายปี
raai bpee

today
วันนี้
wan née

tonight
คืนนี้
keuun née

tomorrow
พรุ่งนี้
prûng née

yesterday
เมื่อวานนี้
mêua waan née

the day after tomorrow
มะรืนนี้
má reuun née

the day before
yesterday
เมื่อวานซืน
mêua waan seuun

on Mondays
ทุกวันจันทร์
túk wan jan

every Sunday
ทุกวันอาทิตย์
túk wan aa tít

last Thursday
พฤหัสที่แล้ว
pá réu hàt têe láew

next Friday
ศุกร์หน้า
sùk nâa

the week before
อาทิตย์ก่อน
aa tít gòrn

the week after
อาทิตย์ถัดไป
aa tít tàt bpai

in February
ในเดือนกุมภาพันธ์
nai deuan gum paa pan

in 2018
ในปี 2018
nai bpee sŏrng pan sìp
bpàirt

in the '80s
ในทศวรรษ 1980
nai tót sà wát nèung pan
gâao róy bpairt sìp

What day is it?
วันอะไร
wan à rai

What is today's date?
วันนี้วันที่เท่าไหร่
wan née wan têe tâo rài

spring
ฤดูใบไม้ผลิ
réu doo bai máai plì

summer
ฤดูร้อน
réu doo rórn

autumn
ฤดูใบไม้ร่วง
réu doo bai máai rûang

winter
ฤดูหนาว
réu doo năao

in spring
ในฤดูใบไม้ผลิ
nai réu doo bai máai plì

in winter
ในฤดูหนาว
nai réu doo năao

17

How's the weather?
อากาศเป็นยังไง
aa gàat bpen yang ngai

What's the forecast for today/tomorrow?
พยากรณ์อากาศวันนี้/พรุ่งนี้เป็นยังไง
pá yaa gorn aa gàat wan née/prûng née bpen yang ngai

Is it going to rain?
ฝนจะตกไหม
fŏn jà dtòk mái

What a lovely day!
วันนี้อากาศดีจริงๆ
wan née aa gàat dee jing jing

What awful weather!
อากาศแย่จังเลย
aa gàat yâir jang loey

It's sunny.
แดดดี
dàirt dee

It's cloudy.
เมฆครึ้ม
mâyk kréum

It's misty.
มีหมอกสลัว
mee mòrk sà lŭa

It's foggy/stormy.
มีหมอกลง/มีพายุ
mee mòrk long/mee paa yú

It's freezing.
อากาศหนาวจัด
aa gàat nǎao jàt

It's raining/snowing.
ฝน/หิมะ กำลังตก
fŏn/hì má gam lang dtòk

It's windy.
ลมแรง
lom rairng

It is...
อากาศ...
aa gàat...

nice
ดี
dee

horrible
แย่
yâir

hot
ร้อน
rórn

warm
อุ่น
ùn

cool
เย็น
yen

wet
ฝนตกเยอะ
fŏn dtòk yúh

humid
ชื้น
chéuun

mild
กำลังสบาย
gam lang sà baai

hail
ลูกเห็บ
lôok hèp

ice
น้ำแข็ง
nám kěng

gale
ลมพายุ
lom paa yú

thunder
พายุ
paa yú

lightning
ฟ้าแลบ
fáa lâirp

TRANSPORT | การคมนาคมขนส่ง

Transport in Thailand is always improving. If you land at Suvarnabhumi airport in Bangkok, the Airport Rail Link can connect you to the BTS Skytrain and the MRT underground. There are also controlled-access highways with toll booths allowing airport taxis to zip over a large part of the city in a short time. There are many ways to get around the country including regular coach, train, plane, and ferry services.

helicopter
เฮลิคอปเตอร์
hay lí kóp dtêr

rotor
ปีกหมุน
bpèek mǔn

blade
ใบพัด
bai pát

cockpit
ที่นั่งนักบิน
têe nâng nák bin

nose
ส่วนหัวเครื่อง
sùan hǔa krêuang

tail
ส่วนหาง
sùan hǎng

YOU MIGHT SAY...

Excuse me.
ขอโทษครับ/ค่ะ
kŏr tôht kráp/kà

Where is...?
... อยู่ที่ไหน
yòo têe năi

What's the quickest way to...?
ไป ... เร็วที่สุดอย่างไร
bpai ... rew têe sùt yang ngai

Is it far from here?
... อยู่ไกลไหม
yòo glai mái

I'm lost.
ผม/ฉัน หลงทาง
pŏm/chán lŏng taang

Can I walk there?
ผม/ฉัน เดินไปได้ไหม
pŏm/chán dern bpai dâai mái

Is there a bus/train to...?
มีรถบัสหรือรถไฟไป ... ไหม
mee rót bàt rĕeu rót fai bpai ... mái

A single/return ticket, please.
ขอตั๋วเที่ยวเดียว/ไปกลับ ครับ/ค่ะ
kŏr dtŭa tîaw diaw/bpai glàp kráp/kà

YOU MIGHT HEAR...

It's over there.
อยู่ที่นั่น
yòo têe nân

It's in the other direction.
อยู่อีกทางหนึ่ง
yòo èek taang nèung

It's ... minutes away.
อยู่ไกล ... นาที
yòo glai ... naa tee

Go straight ahead.
ตรงไปเลย
dtrong bpai loey

Turn left/right.
เลี้ยวซ้าย/ขวา
líaw sáai/kwăa

It's next to/near to...
อยู่ติดกับ/ใกล้กับ...
yòo dtìt gàp/glâi gàp...

It's opposite...
อยู่ตรงข้ามกับ...
yòo dtrong kâam gàp...

Follow the signs for...
ตามป้ายบอกทางไป...
dtaam bpâai bòrk taang bpai...

VOCABULARY

street
ถนน
tà nǒn

commuter
คนเดินทางไปทำงาน
kon dern taang bpai tam ngaan

driver
คนขับรถ
kon kàp rót

passenger
ผู้โดยสาร
pôo dohy sǎan

pedestrian
คนเดินเท้า
kon dern táao

traffic
การจราจร
gaan jà raa jorn

traffic jam
รถติด
rót dtìt

rush hour
ชั่วโมงเร่งด่วน
chûa mohng râyng dùan

public transport
ขนส่งสาธารณะ
kǒn sòng sǎ taa rá ná

taxi
แท็กซี่
ték sêe

taxi rank
ที่จอดแท็กซี่
têe jòrt ték sêe

directions
เส้นทาง
sên taang

route
เส้นทาง
sên taang

to walk
เดิน
dern

to drive
ขับรถ
kàp rót

to turn
เลี้ยว
líaw

to commute
เดินทางไปทำงาน
dern taang bpai tam ngaan

to take a taxi
นั่งแท็กซี่
nâng ték sêe

YOU SHOULD KNOW...

Cars do not stop at zebra crossings and even at pelican crossings you should be careful. Look out for pedestrian footbridges which can be used to cross the road.

map
แผนที่
pǎirn têe

road sign
ป้ายจราจร
bpâai jà raa jorn

timetable
ตารางเดินรถ
dtaa raang dern rót

In Thailand people drive on the left-hand side of the road like in the UK. Traffic in Bangkok gets very congested and there are a lot of accidents but drivers are usually polite. If you do decide to drive, be sure to keep your passport and driving licence with you.

YOU MIGHT SAY...

Is this the road to...?
ถนนนี้ไป ... ใช่ไหม
tà nǒn née bpai ... châi mái

Can I park here?
ผม/ฉัน จอดรถที่นี่ได้ไหม
pǒm/chán jòrt rót têe nêe dâai mái

Do I have to pay to park?
ผม/ฉัน ต้องจ่ายค่าจอดรถไหม
pǒm/chán dtông jàai kâa jòrt rót mái

Where can I hire a car?
ผม/ฉัน เช่ารถได้ที่ไหน
pǒm/chán châo rót dâai têe nǎi

I'd like to hire a car...
ผม/ฉัน อยากจะเช่ารถ...
pǒm/chán yàak jà châo rót...

... for four days.
... สี่วัน
sèe wan

... for a week.
... หนึ่งอาทิตย์
nèung aa tít

What is your daily/weekly rate?
ค่าเช่า รายวัน/รายอาทิตย์ เท่าไหร่
kâa châo raai wan/raai aa tít tâo rài

When/Where must I return it?
ผม/ฉัน ต้องคืนรถ เมื่อไหร่/ที่ไหน
pǒm/chán dtông keuun rót mêua rài/têe nǎi

Where is the nearest petrol station?
ปั๊มน้ำมัน ใกล้ที่สุดอยู่ที่ไหน
bpám nám man glâi têe sùt yòo têe nǎi

I'd like ... baht of fuel, please.
เติมน้ำมัน ... บาทครับ/ค่ะ
dterm nám man ... bàat kráp/kâ

I'd like ... litres of fuel, please.
เติมน้ำมัน ... ลิตร ครับ/ค่ะ
dterm nám man ... lít kráp/kâ

It's pump number...
ปั๊มเบอร์ ... ครับ/ค่ะ
bpám ber ... kráp/kâ

You can/can't park here.
คุณจอดรถที่นี่ ได้/ไม่ได้
kun jòrt rót têe nêe dâai/mâi dâai

It's free to park here.
ที่นี่จอดรถฟรี
têe nêe jòrt rót free

It costs ... to park here.
ค่าจอดรถที่นี่...
kâa jòrt rót têe nêe...

Car hire is ... per day.
ค่าเช่ารถวันละ...
kâa châo rót wan lá...

May I see your documents, please?
ขอดูใบขับขี่หน่อย ครับ/ค่ะ
kǒr doo bai kàp kèe nòy kráp/kâ

Please return it to...
ช่วยเอารถไปคืนที่...
chûay ao rót bpai keuun têe

Please return the car with a full tank of fuel.
ช่วยเติมน้ำมันเต็มถังตอนคืนรถ
chûay dterm nám man dtem tǎng dtorn keuun rót

Which pump are you at?
ปั๊มคุณเบอร์อะไร
bpám kun ber à rai

How much fuel would you like?
เติมน้ำมันเท่าไหร่ครับ/คะ
dterm nám man tâo rài kráp/kâ

VOCABULARY

people carrier มินิแวน mí ní wairn	driver's seat ที่นั่งคนขับ têe nâng kon kàp	engine เครื่องยนต์ krêuang yon
caravan รถคาราวาน rót kaa raa waan	back seat ที่นั่งด้านหลัง têe nâng dâan lăng	automatic อัตโนมัติ àt dtà noh mát
motorhome รถบ้าน rót bâan	child seat ที่นั่งสำหรับเด็ก têe nâng sǎm ràp dèk	electric ไฟฟ้า fai fáa
passenger seat ที่นั่งผู้โดยสาร têe nâng pôo dohy sǎan	sunroof หลังคารับแสง lǎng kaa ráp sǎirng	hybrid ไฮบริด hai brìt

battery	fuel tank	to park
แบตเตอรี	ถังน้ำมัน	จอด
bèt dter rêe	tăng nám man	jòrt

brake	gearbox	to reverse
เบรก	เกียร์	ถอยหลัง
bràyk	gia	tŏy lăng

accelerator	Breathalyser®	to slow down
คันเร่ง	เครื่องวัดแอลกอฮอล์	ลดความเร็ว
kan râyng	จากลมหายใจ	lót kwaam rew
	krêuang wát airn gor	
	horn jàak lom hăai jai	

air conditioning	transmission	to speed
เครื่องปรับอากาศ	การส่งกำลัง	เร่งความเร็ว
krêuang bpràp aa gàat	gaan sòng gam lang	râyng kwaam rew

clutch	to brake	to start the engine
คลัตช์	หยุด	สตาร์ทเครื่อง
klát	yùt	sà dtàat krêuang

exhaust (pipe)	to overtake	to stop
(ท่อ)ไอเสีย	แซง	หยุด
(tôr) ai sĭa	sairng	yùt

YOU SHOULD KNOW...

Car rental companies are likely to ask for an international driving licence.

INTERIOR

dashboard
แผงหน้ารถ
păirng nâa rót

fuel gauge
ตัววัดน้ำมัน
dtua wát nám man

gearstick
เกียร์กระปุก
gia grà bpùk

glove compartment
ลิ้นชักหน้ารถ
lín chák nâa rót

handbrake
เบรกมือ
bràyk meuu

headrest
ที่พิงศีรษะ
têe ping sĕe sà

ignition
กุญแจสตาร์ท
gun jair sà dtáat

rearview mirror
กระจกมองหลัง
grà jòk morng lăng

sat nav
เครื่องนำทาง
krêuang nam taang

seatbelt
เข็มขัดนิรภัย
kěm kàt ní rá pai

speedometer
ตัววัดความเร็ว
dtua wát kwaam rew

steering wheel
พวงมาลัย
puang maa lai

boot
กระโปรงหลัง
grà bprohng lăng

roof
หลังคา
lăng kaa

door
ประตู
bprà dtoo

window
หน้าต่าง
nâa dtàang

wing
บังโคลนข้าง
bang klohn kâang

wheel
ล้อ
lór

tyre
ยางรถ
yaang rót

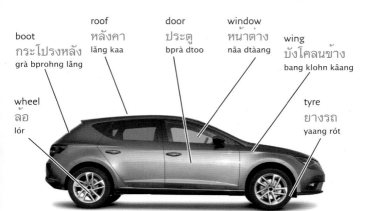

windscreen
กระจกหน้า
grà jòk nâa

windscreen wiper
ที่ปัดน้ำฝน
têe bpàt nám fŏn

wing mirror
กระจกมองข้าง
grà jòk morng kâang

bonnet
กระโปรงหน้า
grà bprohng nâa

headlight
ไฟหน้า
fai nâa

bumper
กันชน
gan chon

indicator
ไฟเลี้ยว
fai líaw

number plate
ป้ายทะเบียนรถ
bpâai tá bian rót

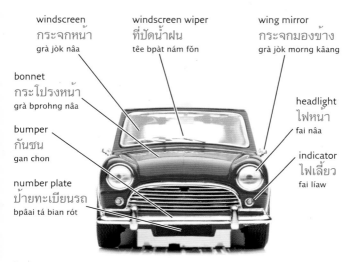

It is legal to drive with a UK licence but you may be asked for an international licence if you want to rent a car. Although traffic gets hectic in Bangkok, the same is not true of the rest of the country. You can break your journey at motorway services which offer good food and coffee.

VOCABULARY

tarmac®
ยางมะตอย
yaang má dtoy

corner
หัวมุม
hŭa mum

exit
ทางออก
taang òrk

slip road
ทางเข้า/ออกถนน
หลัก
taang kâo/ork tà nŏn làk

layby
ที่จอดรถข้างถนน
têe jòrt rót kâang tà nŏn

speed limit
จำกัดความเร็ว
jam gàt kwaam rew

diversion
ทางเบี่ยง
taang bìang

roadworks
ทำถนน
àŏ

parking meter
เครื่องเก็บค่าจอดรถ
êeâòó

driving licence
ใบขับขี่
bai kàp kèe

car registration document
คู่มือทะเบียนรถ
kôo meuu tá bian rót

car insurance
ประกันภัยรถยนต์
bprà gan pai rót yon

car hire/rental
รถเช่า
rót châo

unleaded petrol
น้ำมันไร้สารตะกั่ว
nám man rái săan dtà gùa

diesel
น้ำมันดีเซล
nám man dee sayn

YOU SHOULD KNOW...

Speed limits on Thai roads go by kmph, not mph. The speed limits for different types of roads are:
motorways – 120 kmph
rural – 90 kmph
urban – 80 kmph.
There are exceptions to the above so look out for the speed limit signs.

bridge
สะพาน
sà paan

car park
ที่จอดรถ
têe jòrt rót

car wash
เครื่องล้างรถ
krêuang láang rót

fuel pump
หัวจ่ายน้ำมัน
hǔa jàai nám man

junction
ทางแยก
taang yâirk

kerb
ขอบถนน
kòrp tà nǒn

lane
เลน
layn

motorway
มอเตอร์เวย์
mor dter way

parking space
ช่องจอดรถ
chông jòrt rót

pavement
ทางเท้า
taang táao

petrol station
ปั๊มน้ำมัน
bpám nám man

pothole
หลุม
lǔm

road
ถนน
tà nŏn

speed camera
กล้องตรวจจับความเร็ว
glông dtrùat jàp kwaam
rew

ticket machine
เครื่องขายตั๋ว
krêuang kăai dtŭa

toll point
ด่านเก็บเงิน
dàan gèp nguhn

traffic cone
กรวยจราจร
gruay jà raa jorn

traffic lights
ไฟจราจร
fai jà raa jorn

traffic police
ตำรวจจราจร
dtam rùat jà raa jorn

tunnel
อุโมงค์
ù mohng

zebra crossing
ทางม้าลาย
taang máa laai

29

CAR TROUBLE | ปัญหารถยนต์

If you break down on the motorway, call either the police or the breakdown service. Otherwise, you can call 122 to contact the emergency services. To guarantee an English-speaking operator you can always call the tourist police on 1155.

YOU MIGHT SAY...

Can you help me?
คุณช่วย ผม/ฉัน หน่อยได้ไหม
kun chûay pǒm/chán nòy dâai mái

I've broken down.
ผม/ฉัน รถเสีย
pǒm/chán rót sǐa

I've had an accident.
ผม/ฉัน เกิดอุบัติเหตุ
pǒm/chán gèrt ù bàt dtì hàyt

I've run out of petrol.
ผม/ฉัน น้ำมันหมด
pǒm/chán nám man mòt

I've got a flat tyre.
ผม/ฉัน ยางแบน
pǒm/chán yaang bairn

I've lost my car keys.
ผม/ฉัน ทำกุญแจรถหาย
pǒm/chán tam gun jair rót hǎi

The car won't start.
รถสตาร์ทไม่ติด
rót sà dtáat mâi dtìt

I've been injured.
ผม/ฉัน บาดเจ็บ
pǒm/chán bàat jèp

Call an ambulance.
เรียกรถพยาบาล
rîak rót pá yaa baan

Can you send a breakdown van?
ช่วยส่งรถลากมาหน่อยได้ไหม
chûay sòng rót lâak maa nòy dâai mái

Is there a garage/petrol station nearby?
แถวนี้มี อู่ซ่อมรถ/ปั๊มน้ำมัน ไหม
tǎew née mee òo sôm rót/bpám nám man mái

Can you tow me to a garage?
คุณช่วยลากรถไปที่อู่ได้ไหม
kun chûay lâak rót bpai têe òo dâai mái

Can you help me change this wheel?
คุณช่วยเปลี่ยนล้อรถได้ไหม
kun chûay bplìan lór rót dâai mái

How much will a repair cost?
ค่าซ่อมรถเท่าไหร่
kâa sôm rót tâo rài

When will the car be fixed?
รถจะซ่อมเสร็จเมื่อไหร่
rót jà sôm sèt mêua rài

Do you need any help?
คุณต้องการความช่วยเหลือไหม
kun dtông gaan kwaam chûay lĕua mái

The repairs will cost...
ค่าซ่อมรถ ... บาท
kâa sôm rót ... bàat

Are you hurt?
คุณบาดเจ็บรึเปล่า
kun bàat jèp réu bplàao

We need to order new parts.
เราต้องสั่งอะไหล่มา
rao dtông sàng à lài maa

What's wrong with your car?
รถคุณเป็นอะไร
rót kun bpen à rai

The car will be ready by...
รถจะเสร็จ...
rót jà sèt...

Where have you broken down?
รถคุณเสียอยู่ที่ไหน
rót kun sĭa yòo têe năi

I need your insurance details.
ขอทราบรายละเอียดประกันรถ
kŏr sâap raai lá ìat bprà gan rót

I can give you a jumpstart.
ผม/ฉัน จะช่วยจั๊มแบต
pŏm/chán jà chûay jám bèt

Do you have your driving licence?
คุณมีใบขับขี่ไหม
kun mee bai kàp kèe mái

VOCABULARY

accident	mechanic	to have a flat tyre
อุบัติเหตุ	ช่างยนต์	มียางแบน
ù bàt dtì hàyt	châng yon	mee yaang bairn
breakdown	garage	to change a tyre
รถเสีย	อู่ซ่อมรถ	เปลี่ยนยาง
rót sĭa	òo sôm rót	bplìan yaang
collision	to break down	to tow
รถชนกัน	รถเสีย	ลาก
rót chon gan	rót sĭa	lâak
flat tyre	to have an accident	to repair
ยางแบน	เกิดอุบัติเหตุ	ซ่อม
yaang bairn	gèrt ù bàt dtì hàyt	sôm

airbag
ถุงลมนิรภัย
tŭng lom ní rá pai

antifreeze
ยากันน้ำแข็ง
yaa gan nám kěng

checkpoint
ด่านตรวจ
dàan dtrùat

garage
อู่ซ่อมรถ
òo sôm rót

jack
แม่แรง
mâir rairng

jump leads
สายจั๊มแบต
săai jám bèt

spare wheel
ล้ออะไหล่
lór à lài

tow truck
รถลาก
rót lâak

tyre pump
ที่เติมลม
têe dterm lom

YOU SHOULD KNOW...

The narrow alleyways of Bangkok can pose a challenge even to local drivers. Trying to navigate them in a car is not recommended unless you know what you're doing!

Local bus routes in Bangkok are difficult to navigate for foreigners. The main stops are written on the side of the bus in Thai script. Fares are collected by a conductor who walks up and down the bus. If you want to give them a go, it is possible to buy a route map and check which route number goes to your destination. For intercity travel there are plenty of long-distance coaches and air-conditioned tour buses which are comfortable and easy to book.

YOU MIGHT SAY...

Is there a bus to...?
มีรถบัสไป ... ไหม
mee rót bàt bpai ... mái

When is the next bus to...?
รถไป ... คันต่อไปเมื่อไหร่
rót bpai ... kan dtòr bpai mêua rài

Which bus goes to the city centre?
รถบัสสายไหนไปใจกลางเมือง
rót bàt săi năi bpai jai glaang meuang

Where is the bus stop?
ป้ายรถเมล์อยู่ที่ไหน
bpâai rót may yòo têe năi

Which stand does the coach leave from?
รถออกจากท่าไหน
rót òok jàak tâa năi

How frequent are buses to...?
รถไป ... มีกี่เที่ยว
rót bpai ... mee gèe tîaw

Where can I buy tickets?
ผม/ฉัน ซื้อตั๋วได้ที่ไหน
pŏm/chán séu dtŭa dâai têe năi

How much is it to go to...?
ไป ... เท่าไหร่
bpai ... tâo rài

A full/half fare, please.
ขอตั๋ว เต็ม/ครึ่งราคา ครับ/ค่ะ
kŏr dtŭa dtem/krêung raa kaa/krúp/kâ

Could you tell me when to get off?
ช่วยบอกได้ไหมว่าลงตรงไหน
chûay bòrk dâai mái wâa long dtrong năi

How many stops is it?
ไปอีกกี่ป้าย
bpai èek gèe bpâai

I want to get off at the next stop, please.
ผม/ฉัน ขอลงป้ายหน้า ครับ/ค่ะ
pŏm/chán kŏr long bpâai nâa krúp/kâ

YOU SHOULD KNOW...

Outside Bangkok, converted pick-ups trucks with two rows of benches in the back (known as "sŏrng tăew") serve as local buses.

The number 17 goes to...
สาย 17 ไป...
săai sìp jèt bpai...

The bus stop is down the road.
ป้ายรถเมล์อยู่หลังจากนี้
bpâai rót may yòo lăng jàak née

It leaves from stand 21.
รถออกจากท่าเบอร์ 21
rót òrk jàak tâa ber yêe sìp èt

You can/can't buy tickets on the bus.
คุณซื้อตั๋วบนรถ ได้/ไม่ได้
kun séuu dtŭa bon rót dâai mâi dâai

You buy tickets at the machine/office.
คุณซื้อตั๋วที่ เครื่องขายตั๋ว/สำนักงาน
kun séuu dtŭa têe krêuang kăai dtŭa/săm nák ngaan

VOCABULARY

bus route
เส้นทางเดินรถ
sên taang dern rót

bus lane
บัสเลน
bàt layn

bus pass
บัตรโดยสารรถบัส
bàt dohy săan rót bàt

bus station
สถานีรถขนส่ง
sà tăa nee rót kŏn sòng

bus stop
ป้ายรถเมล์
bpâai rót may

fare
ค่ารถ
kâa rót

full/half fare
เต็ม/ครึ่ง ราคา
dtem/krêung raa kaa

concession
สิทธิประโยชน์
sìt tí bprà yòht

shuttle bus
รถรับส่ง
rót ráp sòng

school bus
รถโรงเรียน
rót rohng rian

airport bus
รถรับส่งสนามบิน
rót ráp sòng sà năam bin

to catch the bus
ไปขึ้นรถโดยสาร
bpai kêun rót dohy săan

bus
รถเมล์/รถบัส
rót may/rót bàt

coach
รถโดยสาร
rót dohy săan

minibus
รถตู้
rót dtôo

Motorbikes and scooters play an important role for people in Thailand as a way of getting around. There are also motorbike taxis which are a convenient way to weave through traffic jams and narrow alleyways. However, rented scooters are also a common way for tourists to get seriously hurt, so drive carefully!

VOCABULARY

motorcyclist
คนขี่รถจักรยานยนต์
kon kèe rót jàk grà yaan yon

fuel tank
ถังน้ำมัน
tăng nám man

mudguard
บังโคลน
bang klohn

scooter
รถมอเตอร์ไซค์เกียร์
ออโต้
rót mor dter sai gia or dtôh

handlebars
แฮนด์จับ
hairn jàp

kickstand
ขาตั้ง
kăa dtâng

seat
เบาะ
bò

headlight
ไฟหน้า
fai nâa

exhaust pipe
ท่อไอเสีย
tôr ai sĭa

boots
รองเท้าบูท
rorng táao bòot

crash helmet
หมวกกันน็อค
mùak gan nók

helmet cam
กล้องติดหมวกกันน็อค
glông dtìt mùak gan nók

leather gloves
ถุงมือหนัง
tŭng meuu năng

leather jacket
เสื้อหนัง
sêua năng

motorbike
บิ๊กไบค์
bìk bái

BICYCLE | จักรยาน

In some tourist destinations in Thailand (such as Chiang Mai or Ayutthaya) it is possible to hire bicycles to explore the area. The prices tend to be very reasonable.

YOU MIGHT SAY...

Where can I hire a bicycle?
ผม/ฉัน เช่าจักรยานได้ที่ไหน
pǒm/chán châo jàk grà yaan dâai têe nǎi

How much is it to hire?
ค่าเช่าจักรยานเท่าไหร่
kâa châo jàk grà yaan tâo rài

My bike has a puncture.
จักรยานของ ผม/ฉัน ยางรั่ว
jàk grà yaan kǒrng pǒm/chán yaang rûa

YOU MIGHT HEAR...

Bike hire is ... per day/week.
ค่าเช่าจักรยานราคา ... ต่อ วัน/อาทิตย์
kâa châo jàk grà yaan raa kaa ... dtòr wan/aa tít

You must wear a helmet.
คุณต้องใส่หมวกกันน็อค
kun dtông sài mùak gan nók

There's a cycle path from ... to...
มีทางจักรยานจาก ... ถึง...
mee taang jàk grà yaan jàak ... těung...

VOCABULARY

cyclist
คนขี่จักรยาน
kon kèe jàk grà yaan

mountain bike
จักรยานเสือภูเขา
jàk grà yaan sěua poo kǎo

road bike
จักรยานสำหรับถนน
jàk grà yaan sǎm ràp tà nǒn

bike stand
ที่จอดรถจักรยาน
têe jòrt rót jàk grà yaan

child seat
ที่นั่งเด็ก
têe nâng dèk

cycle lane/path
เลนจักรยาน
layn jàk grà yaan

to get a puncture
ยางรั่ว
yaang rûa

to cycle
ขี่จักรยาน
kèe jàk grà yaan

to go for a bike ride
ไปขี่จักรยาน
bpai kèe jàk grà yaan

bell
กระดิ่ง
grà dìng

bike lock
โซ่ล็อคจักรยาน
sôh lók jàk grà yaan

front light
ไฟหน้า
fai nâa

helmet
หมวกกันน็อคจักรยาน
mùak gan nók jàk grà
yaan

pump
ปั๊มลมยาง
bpám lom yaang

reflector
ไฟหลัง
fai lăng

BICYCLE

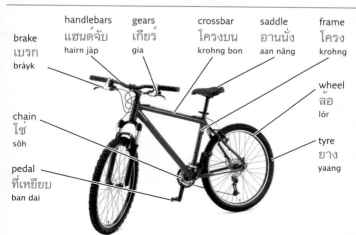

brake
เบรก
bràyk

handlebars
แฮนด์จับ
hairn jàp

gears
เกียร์
gia

crossbar
โครงบน
krohng bon

saddle
อานนั่ง
aan nâng

frame
โครง
krohng

wheel
ล้อ
lór

chain
โซ่
sôh

tyre
ยาง
yaang

pedal
ที่เหยียบ
ban dai

37

RAIL TRAVEL | การเดินทางโดยรถไฟ

Train travel, with stunning views of the countryside and local vendors walking through the carriages, can be an exciting experience. Tickets are easy to book at the station and sleeper carriages are available for long-distance journeys.

YOU MIGHT SAY...

Is there a train to...?
มีรถไฟไป ... ไหม
mee rót fai bpai ... mái

When is the next train to...?
รถไฟไป ... ขบวนต่อไปเมื่อไหร่
rót fai bpai ... kà buan dtòr bpai mêua rài

Where is the nearest train station?
สถานีรถไฟใกล้ที่สุดอยู่ที่ไหน
sà tăa nee rót fai glâi têe sùt yòo têe năi

Which platform does it leave from?
ชานชาลาไหนที่รถไฟออก
chaan chaa laa năi têe rót fai òrk

Which line do I take for...?
ผม/ฉัน ขึ้นรถไฟสายไหนไป...
pŏm/chán kêun rót fai săai năi bpai...

A ticket to..., please.
ซื้อตั๋วไป ... ครับ/ค่ะ
séuu dtŭa bpai ... kráp/kâ

I'd like to reserve a seat/couchette, please.
ผม/ฉัน อยากจอง ที่นั่ง/รถนอน ครับ/ค่ะ
pŏm/chán yàak jorng têe nâng/rót norn kráp/kâ

Do I have to change?
ผม/ฉัน ต้องเปลี่ยนขบวนรถไหม
pŏm/chán dtông bplìan kà buan rót mái

Where do I change for...?
ผม/ฉัน เปลี่ยนขบวนรถไป ... ที่ไหน
pŏm/chán bplìan kà buan rót bpai ... têe năi

Where is platform 4?
ชานชาลา 4 อยู่ที่ไหน
chaan chaa laa sèe yòo têe năi

Is this the right platform for...?
ชานชาลานี้ไป ... ใช่ไหม
chaan chaa laa née bpai ... châi mái

Is this the train for...?
รถไฟขบวนนี้ไป ... ใช่ไหม
rót fai kà buan née bpai ... châi mái

Is this seat free?
ที่นั่งนี้ว่างไหม
têe nâng née wâang mái

Where is the restaurant car?
ตู้เสบียงอยู่ที่ไหน
dtôo sà biang yòo têe năi

I've missed my train!
ผม/ฉัน ตกรถไฟ
pŏm/chán dtòk rót fai

YOU MIGHT HEAR...

The next train leaves at...
รถขบวนต่อไปออกเวลา...
rót kà buan dtòr bpai òrk way laa...

Would you like a single or return ticket?
คุณอยากได้ตั๋วเที่ยวเดียวหรือไปกลับ
kun yàak dâai dtŭa tîaw diaw rĕuu bpai glàp

Would you like a first-class or a second-class ticket?
คุณต้องการตั๋วชั้นหนึ่งหรือชั้นสอง
kun dtông gaan dtŭa chán nèung rĕuu chán sŏrng

Would you like a first-class or a second-class sleeper?
คุณต้องการตู้นอนชั้นหนึ่งหรือชั้นสอง
kun dtông gaan dtôo norn chán nèung rĕuu chán sŏrng kráp

I'm sorry, this journey is fully booked.
ขอโทษ ครับ/ค่ะ รถเที่ยวนี้เต็มหมดแล้ว
kŏr tôht kráp/kâ rót tîaw née dtem mòt láew

You must change at...
คุณต้องเปลี่ยนรถที่...
kun dtông bplìan rót têe...

Platform 4 is down there.
ชานชาลาที่ 4 อยู่ทางนั้น
chaan chaa laa têe sèe yòo taang nán

This is the right train/platform.
นี่คือขบวนรถไฟ/ชานชาลาที่ถูก
nêe keuu kà buan rót fai/chaan chaa laa têe tòok

You have to go to platform 2.
คุณต้องไปที่ชานชาลา 2
kun dtông bpai chaan chaa laa sŏrng

This seat is free/taken.
ที่นั่งนี้ ว่าง/มีคนนั่ง
têe nâng née wâang/mee kon nâng

The restaurant car is in coach 8.
ตู้เสบียงคือรถขบวนที่ 8
dtôo sà biang keuu rót kà buan têe bpàirt

The next stop is...
สถานีต่อไป...
sà tăa nee dtòr bpai...

Change here for...
เปลี่ยนรถที่นี่เพื่อไป...
bplian rót têe nêe pêua bpai...

VOCABULARY

rail network
เส้นทางรถไฟ
sên taang rót fai

high-speed train
รถไฟความเร็วสูง
rót fai kwaam rew sŏong

passenger train
รถไฟโดยสาร
rót fai dohy săan

freight train
รถไฟขนสินค้า
rót fai kŏn sĭn káa

coach
ขบวน
kà buan

train station
สถานีรถไฟ
sà tăa nee rót fai

sleeper
รถนอน
rót norn

porter
คนขนของ
kon kŏn kŏrng

left luggage
ที่ฝากกระเป๋า
têe fàak grà bpăo

first class
ชั้นหนึ่ง
chán nèung

railway police
ตำรวจรถไฟ
dtam rùat rót fai

single ticket
ตั๋วเที่ยวเดียว
dtŭa tîaw diaw

second-class
ชั้นสอง
chán sŏrng

line
สาย
săai

to change trains
เปลี่ยนขบวนรถ
bplìan kà buan rót

YOU SHOULD KNOW...

When travelling by train, be sure to allow extra time for your journey as delays are common.

airport rail link
รถไฟฟ้าแอร์พอร์ต
เรล ลิงก์
rót fai fáa air pórt rayn líng

BTS Skytrain
รถไฟฟ้าบีทีเอส
rót fai fáa bee tee áyt

carriage
รถนั่ง
rót nâng

couchette
รถนอน
rót norn

departure board
ป้ายบอกเวลา
bpâai bòrk way laa

locomotive
หัวรถจักร
hŭa rót jàk

luggage rack
ชั้นวางกระเป๋า
chán waang grà bpǎo

network map
แผนที่เส้นทาง
pǎirn têe sên taang

platform
ชานชาลา
chaan chaa laa

restaurant car
ตู้เสบียง
dtôo sà biang

signal box
ป้อมสัญญาณรถไฟ
bpôm sǎn yaan rót fai

ticket
ตั๋ว
dtǔa

ticket barrier
ประตูอัตโนมัติ
bprà dtôo àt dtà noh mát

ticket machine
เครื่องขายตั๋ว
krêuang kǎai dtǔa

ticket office
ห้องขายตั๋ว
hông kǎai dtǔa

track
รางรถไฟ
raang rót fai

train
รถไฟ
rót fai

train station
สถานีรถไฟ
sà tǎa nee rót fai

Travelling by air is a convenient way to reach certain parts of the country and tickets for domestic flights are usually very reasonably priced. The major airports are comfortable and have good facilities.

YOU MIGHT SAY...

I'm looking for check-in/my gate.

ผม/ฉัน กำลังหาเคาน์เตอร์ เช็ค
อิน/เกท

pŏm/chán gam lang hăa káo dtêr chék in/gàyt

I'm checking in one case.

ผม/ฉัน เช็คอินกระเป๋าเดินทาง
หนึ่งใบ

pŏm/chán chék in grà bpăo dern taang nèung bai

Which gate does the plane leave from?

เครื่องบินออกจากเกทไหน

krêuang bin òrk jàak gàyt năi

When does the gate open/close?

เกท เปิด/ปิด เมื่อไหร่

gàyt bpèrt/bpìt mêua rài

Is the flight on time?

เที่ยวบินตรงเวลาไหม

tîaw bin dtrong way laa mái

I would like a window/an aisle seat, please.

ผม/ฉัน ขอที่นั่ง ริมหน้าต่าง/
ติดทางเดิน ครับ/ค่ะ

pŏm/chán kŏr têe nâng rim nâa dtàang/dtìt taang dern kráp/kâ

I've lost my luggage.

กระเป๋าเดินทางของ ผม/ฉัน
หาย

grà bpăo dern taang kŏrng pŏm/chán hăai

My flight has been delayed.

เที่ยวบินของ ผม/ฉัน ดีเลย์

tîaw bin kŏrng pŏm/chán dee lay

I've missed my connecting flight.

ผม/ฉัน ต่อเครื่องไม่ทัน

pŏm/chán dtòr krêuang mâi tan

Is there a shuttle bus service?

มีบริการรถบัสรับส่งไหม

mee bor rí gaan rót bàt ráp sòng mái

YOU MIGHT HEAR...

Check-in has opened for flight...

เช็คอินเปิดสำหรับเที่ยวบิน...

chék in bpèrt săm ràp tîaw bin...

Is this your bag?

นี่กระเป๋าของคุณใช่ไหม

nêe grà bpăo kŏrng kun châi mái

How many bags are you checking in?

คุณเช็คอินกระเป๋ากี่ใบ

kun chék in grà bpăo gèe bai

Your luggage exceeds the maximum weight.

กระเป๋าของคุณน้ำหนักเกิน

grà bpăo kŏrng kun nám nàk gern

Please go to gate number...

ไปที่เกทหมายเลข ... ครับ/ค่ะ

bpai têe gàyt măai lâyk ... kráp/kâ

Your flight is on time/delayed/cancelled.

เที่ยวบินของคุณ ตรงเวลา/ดีเลย์/ยกเลิก

tîaw bin kŏrng kun dtrong way laa/dee lay/yók lêrk

May I see your ticket/passport, please?

ขอดู ตั๋ว/หนังสือเดินทาง ของคุณหน่อย ครับ/ค่ะ

kŏr doo dtŭa/nang sĕuu dern taang kŏrng kun nòy kráp/kâ

Flight ... is now ready for boarding.

เที่ยวบิน ... พร้อมให้ขึ้นเครื่องแล้ว

tîaw bin ... prórm hâi kêun krêuang láew

Last call for passenger...

เรียกขึ้นเครื่องครั้งสุดท้ายผู้โดยสารนามว่า...

rîak kêun krêuang kráng sùt táai pôo dohy săan naam wâa...

airline
สายการบิน
săai gaan bin

flight
เที่ยวบิน
tîaw bin

Arrivals/Departures
ขาเข้า/ขาออก
kăa kâo/kăa òrk

security
ตรวจความปลอดภัย
dtrùat kwaam bplòrt pai

passport control
การตรวจหนังสือเดินทาง
gaan dtrùat nang sĕuu dern taang

customs
ดานศุลกากร
dàan sŭn lá gaa gorn

cabin crew
ลูกเรือ
lôok reua

business class
ชั้นธุรกิจ
chán tú rá git

economy class
ชั้นประหยัด
chán bprà yàt

aisle
ทางเดิน
taang dern

seatbelt
เข็มขัดนิรภัย
kĕm kàt ní rá pai

tray table
ถาดหน้าที่นั่ง
tàat nâa têe nâng

overhead locker
ที่เก็บของเหนือ
ศีรษะ
têe gèp kŏrng nĕua sĕe sà

wing
ปีก
bpèek

fuselage
ลำตัวเครื่องบิน
lam dtua krêuang bin

engine
เครื่องยนต์
krêuang yon

hold
ห้องเก็บสัมภาระ
hông gèp săm paa rá

hold luggage
สัมภาระในห้องเก็บ
săm paa rá nai hông gèp

hand luggage
สัมภาระติดตัวขึ้น
เครื่อง
săm paa rá dtìt dtua
kêun krêuang

excess baggage
กระเป๋าน้ำหนักเกิน
grà bpăo nám nàk gern

connecting flight
เที่ยวบินต่อ
tîaw bin dtòr

jetlag
อาการเมาเวลา
aa gaan mao way laa

to check in (online)
เช็คอิน (ออนไลน์)
chék in (oon lai)

aeroplane
เครื่องบิน
krêuang bin

airport
สนามบิน
sà năam bin

baggage reclaim
รับสัมภาระ
ráp săm paa rá

boarding card
บัตรโดยสารเครื่องบิน
bàt dohy săan krêuang bin

cabin
ห้องโดยสาร
hông dohy săan

check-in desk
เคาน์เตอร์เช็คอิน
kao dtêr chék in

cockpit
ห้องนักบิน
hông nák bin

duty-free shop
ร้านปลอดภาษี
ráan bplòrt paa sĕe

holdall
กระเป๋าเสื้อผ้า
grà bpăo sêua pâa

information board
ป้ายแสดงเที่ยวบิน
bpâai sà dairng tîaw bin

luggage trolley
รถเข็นสัมภาระ
rót kĕn săm paa rá

passport
หนังสือเดินทาง
nang sĕuu dern taang

pilot
นักบิน
nák bin

runway
ลานบิน
laan bin

suitcase
กระเป๋าเดินทาง
grà bpăo dern taang

terminal
อาคารผู้โดยสาร
aa kaan pôo dohy săan

45

Ferry and boat services are the main way of getting to the many offshore islands which are popular with tourists. In addition, the riverboats and ferries in Bangkok are a pleasant means of travel and also offer a way to avoid traffic.

YOU MIGHT SAY...

When is the next boat to...?
เรือไป ... ลำต่อไปกี่โมง
reua bpai ... lam dtòr bpai gèe mohng

Where does the boat leave from?
เรือออกจากที่ไหน
reua òrk jàak têe nǎi

What time is the last boat to...?
เรือไป ... ลำสุดท้ายกี่โมง
reua bpai ... lam sùt táai gèe mohng

How long is the trip/crossing?
ใช้เวลา เดินทาง/ข้ามฟาก นาน แค่ไหน
chái way laa dern taang/kâam fâak naan kâir nǎi

How many crossings a day are there?
มีเรือไปวันละกี่เที่ยว
mee reua bpai wan lá gèe tîaw

How much for ... passengers?
ค่าตั๋วสำหรับ ... คนเท่าไหร่
kâa dtŭa sǎm ràp ... kon tâo rài

How much is it for a vehicle?
ค่าตั๋วของรถยนต์เท่าไหร่
kâa dtŭa kǒng rót yon tâo rài

I feel seasick.
ผม/ฉัน เมาเรือ
pǒm/chán mao reua

YOU MIGHT HEAR...

The boat leaves from...
เรือออกจาก...
reua òrk jàak...

The trip/crossing lasts...
ใช้เวลา เดินทาง/ข้ามฟาก...
chái way laa dern taang/kâam fâak...

There are ... crossings a day.
มีเรือข้าม ... เที่ยวต่อวัน
mee reua kâam ... tîaw dtòr wan

The ferry is delayed/cancelled.
เรือ ดีเลย์/ยกเลิกแล้ว
reua dee lay/yók lêrk láew

Sea conditions are good/bad.
สภาพคลื่นลม ดี/ไม่ดี
sà pâap klêuun lom dee/mâi dee

harbour
ท่าเรือ
tâa reua

port
ท่าเรือ
tâa reua

ferry
เรือข้ามฟาก
reua kâam fâak

ferry crossing
เส้นทางเรือข้ามฟาก
sên taang reua kâam fâak

ferry terminal
ที่พักผู้โดยสารเรือ
ข้ามฟาก
têe pák pôo dohy săan
reua kâam fâak

car deck
ส่วนจอดรถ
sùan jòrt rót

coastguard
ยามชายฝั่ง
yaam chaai fàng

captain
กัปตัน/คนขับเรือ
gàp dtan/kon kàp reua

crew
ลูกเรือ
lôok reua

to board
ลงเรือ
long reua

to sail
แล่นเรือ
lên reua

to dock
จอดเรือ
jòrt reua

GENERAL

anchor
สมอ
sà mŏr

buoy
ทุ่น
tûn

gangway
สะพานขึ้นเรือ
sà paan kêun reua

jetty
ท่าเรือ
tâa reua

lifebuoy
ทุ่นชูชีพ
tûn choo chêep

lifejacket
เสื้อชูชีพ
sêua choo chêep

FERRY

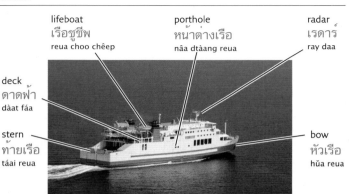

lifeboat
เรือชูชีพ
reua choo chêep

porthole
หน้าต่างเรือ
nâa dtàang reua

radar
เรดาร์
ray daa

deck
ดาดฟ้า
dàat fáa

stern
ท้ายเรือ
táai reua

bow
หัวเรือ
hŭa reua

OTHER BOATS

canal boat
เรือโดยสารในคลอง
reua dohy săan nai klorng

inflatable dinghy
เรือยาง
reua yaang

liner
เรือเดินสมุทร
reua dern sà mùt

sailing boat
เรือใบ
reua bai

trawler
เรือประมงขนาด
ใหญ่
reua brà mong kà nàat yài

yacht
เรือยอช์ท
reua yórt

IN THE HOME | เรื่องของบ้าน

Thailand attracts huge numbers of tourists and expats looking for a place to call their "home" for a time, whether it's for a holiday or for a longer-term stay. This could be a holiday villa near the sea or a high-rise apartment in the city centre.

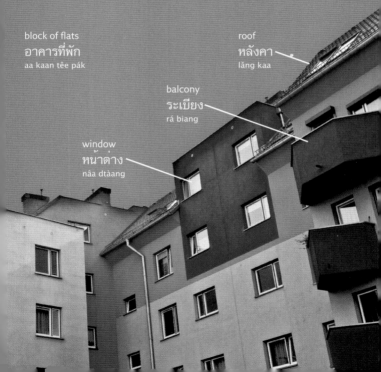

block of flats
อาคารที่พัก
aa kaan têe pák

roof
หลังคา
lăng kaa

balcony
ระเบียง
rá biang

window
หน้าต่าง
nâa dtàang

Lifestyles and living arrangements in urban and rural areas can be very different. Cities have a lot of apartment blocks and terraced houses. In more rural areas, traditional Thai wooden houses are raised up on stilts but these are now being replaced by spacious brick or concrete houses with tiled floors.

YOU MIGHT SAY...

I live in.../I'm staying at...
ผม/ฉัน อยู่ที่... / ผม/ฉัน พักอยู่ที่...
pŏm/chán yòo têe... / pŏm/chán pák yòo têe...

My address is...
ที่อยู่ของ ผม/ฉัน คือ...
têe yòo kŏrng pŏm/chán keuu...

I have a flat/house.
ผม/ฉัน มี คอนโด/บ้าน
pŏm/chán mee korn doh/bâan

I'm the homeowner/tenant.
ผม/ฉัน เป็น เจ้าของบ้าน/ผู้เช่า
pŏm/chán bpen jâo kŏrng bâan/pôo châo

I don't like this area.
ผม/ฉัน ไม่ชอบแถวนี้
pŏm/chán mâi chôrp tăew née

I'd like to buy/rent a property here.
ผม/ฉัน อยากจะ ซื้อ/เช่า ที่พักอาศัยที่นี่
pŏm/chán yàak jà séuu/châo têe pák aa săi têe nêe

YOU MIGHT HEAR...

Where do you live?
คุณอยู่ที่ไหน
kun yòo têe năi

Where are you staying?
คุณพักอยู่ที่ไหน
kun pák yòo têe năi

How long have you lived here?
คุณอยู่ที่นี่นานแค่ไหน
kun yòo têe nêe naan kâir năi

Are you the owner/tenant?
คุณเป็น เจ้าของ/ผู้เช่า ใช่ไหม
kun bpen jâo kŏrng/pôo châo châi mái

VOCABULARY

building	address	suburb
ตึก	ที่อยู่	ชานเมือง
dtèuk	têe yòo	chaan meuang

estate agent	neighbour	to rent
นายหน้าบ้านและที่ดิน	เพื่อนบ้าน	เช่า
naai nâa bâan lé têe din	pêuan bâan	châo

landlord/landlady	rent	to own
เจ้าของบ้าน	ค่าเช่า	เป็นเจ้าของ
jâo kŏrng bâan	kâa châo	bpen jâo kŏrng

tenant	holiday let	to move house
ผู้เช่า	บ้านพักตากอากาศ	ย้ายบ้าน
pôo châo	bâan pák dtàk aa gàat	yáai bâan

YOU SHOULD KNOW...

Foreign nationals are not allowed to buy land. However, it is possible to buy an apartment. A more luxurious high-rise apartment is known in Thai as a "condo", from the American term "condominium".

TYPES OF BUILDING

bungalow
บังกะโล
bang gà loh

condo
คอนโด
korn doh

detached house
บ้านเดี่ยว
bâan dìaw

studio flat
ห้องสตูดิโอ
hông sà dtoo dì oh

traditional Thai house
เรือนไทย
reuan tai

villa
วิลล่า
win lâa

51

In addition to apartment blocks, you will also find detached houses and villas in Thailand; either in big cities or in the countryside where farmers build their own properties.

YOU MIGHT SAY...

There's a problem with...
มีปัญหาเรื่อง...
mee bpan hăa rêuang...

... is not working.
... เสีย
sĭa

The drains are blocked.
ท่อน้ำตัน
tôr náam dtan

The boiler has broken.
เครื่องทำน้ำร้อนเสีย
krêuang tam náam rórn sĭa

There's no hot water.
ไม่มีน้ำร้อน
mâi mee náam rórn

We have a power cut.
ไฟดับ
fai dàp

I need a plumber/an electrician.
ผม/ฉัน ต้องการ ช่างประปา/ช่างไฟฟ้า
pŏm/chán dtông gaan châng bprà bpaa/châng fai fáa

Can it be repaired?
มันซ่อมได้ไหม
man sôrm dâai mái

I can smell gas/smoke.
ผม/ฉัน ได้กลิ่น แก๊ส/ควัน
pŏm/chán dâai glìn gáirt/kwan

YOU MIGHT HEAR...

How long has it been broken/leaking?
มัน เสีย/รั่ว นานแค่ไหนแล้ว
man sĭa/rûa naan kâir năi láew

Where is the electricity meter/water meter/fusebox?
มิเตอร์ไฟ/มิเตอร์น้ำ/กล่องตัดไฟ อยู่ที่ไหน
mí dtêr fai/mí dtêr náam/glòng dtàt fai yòo têe năi

Here's a number for a plumber/an electrician.
นี่เบอร์โทร ช่างประปา/ช่างไฟฟ้า
nêe ber toh châng bprà bpaa/châng fai fáa

VOCABULARY

room
ห้อง
hông

adaptor
อะแดปเตอร์
à dèp dtêr

satellite dish
จานดาวเทียม
jaan daao tiam

ceiling
เพดาน
pay daan

socket
ปลั๊กไฟ
bplák fai

back door
ประตูหลัง
bprà dtoo lăng

wall
กำแพง
gam pairng

extension cable
ปลั๊กพ่วง
bplák pûang

skylight
ช่องแสง
chông săirng

floor
พื้น
péuun

electricity
ไฟฟ้า
fai fáa

light bulb
หลอดไฟ
lòrt fai

battery
แบตเตอรี่
bèt dter rêe

air conditioning
เครื่องปรับอากาศ
krêuang bràp aa gàat

to fix
ซ่อม
sôrm

plug
ปลั๊ก
bplák

mosquito screen
มุ้งลวด
múng lûat

to decorate
ตกแต่ง
dtòk dtèng

INSIDE

boiler
เครื่องทำน้ำร้อน
krêuang tam náam rórn

ceiling fan
พัดลมติดเพดาน
pát lom dtìt pay daan

evaporative cooler
พัดลมไอเย็น
pát lom ai yen

fusebox
กล่องตัดไฟ
glòng dtàt fai

meter
มิเตอร์
mí dtêr

security alarm
สัญญาณกันขโมย
săn yaan gan kà mohy

smoke alarm
สัญญาณเตือนไฟไหม้
săn yaan dteuan fai mâai

standing fan
พัดลมตั้งพื้น
pát lom dtâng péuun

thermostat
เทอร์โมสตัท
ter moh sà dtàt

OUTSIDE

roof
หลังคา
lăng kaa

aerial
เสาอากาศ
săo aa gàat

gutter
รางน้ำฝน
raang náam fŏn

drainpipe
ท่อน้ำฝน
tôr náam fŏn

window
หน้าต่าง
nâa dtàang

driveway
ถนนส่วนบุคคล
tà nŏn sùan bùk kon

front door
ประตูหน้า
bprà dtoo nâa

garage
โรงจอดรถ
rohng jòrt rót

54

YOU MIGHT SAY/HEAR...

Would you like to come round?
คุณอยากแวะมาเที่ยวบ้านไหม
kun yàak wé maa tîaw bâan mái

May I come in?
ขอ ผม/ฉัน เข้าไปได้ไหม
kŏr pŏm/chán kâo bpai dâai mái

Hi! Come in.
สวัสดี ครับ/ค่ะ เข้ามาเลย
sà wàt dee kráp/kà kâo maa loey

Shall I take my shoes off?
ให้ ผม/ฉัน ถอดรองเท้าไหม
hâi pŏm/chán tòrt rorng táao mái

Make yourself at home.
ตามสบายเลยนะ
dtaam sà baai loey ná

Can I use your bathroom?
ขอเข้าห้องน้ำหน่อยได้ไหม
ครับ/คะ
kŏr kâo hông náam nòy dâai mái
kráp/kâ

Come round again soon.
แวะมาเที่ยวอีกนะ
wé maa tîaw èek ná

Thanks for inviting me over.
ขอบคุณที่ชวนมานะ
kòrp kun têe chuan maa ná

I like having people over.
ผม/ฉัน ชอบให้คนมาบ้าน
pŏm/chán chôrp hâi kon maa bâan

VOCABULARY

threshold/doorway
ทางเข้าประตู
taang kâo bprà dtoo

coat hook
ตะขอแขวนเสื้อ
dtà kŏr kwâirn sêua

staircase
บันได
ban dai

corridor
ทางเดิน
taang dern

console table
โต๊ะวางของแต่งบ้าน
dtó waang kŏrng dtèng
bâan

banister
ราวบันได
raao ban dai

hallway
ทางเดิน
taang dern

landing
เชิงบันได
cherng ban dai

to buzz somebody in
กดเปิดประตูให้เข้า
gòt bpèrt bprà dtoo hâi
kâo

to come in	to wipe one's feet	to hang one's jacket up
เข้ามา	เช็ดเท้า	แขวนเสื้อ
kâo maa	chét táao	kwǎirn sêua

GENERAL

doorbell
กริ่งประตู
grìng bprà dtoo

door handle
ลูกบิดประตู
lôok bìt bprà dtoo

doormat
พรมเช็ดเท้า
prom chét táao

intercom
อินเตอร์คอม
in dter korm

key
กุญแจ
gun jair

key fob
กุญแจรีโมท
gun jair ree móht

lift
ลิฟต์
líp

shoe cupboard
ตู้เก็บรองเท้า
dtôo gèp rorng táao

stairwell
ช่องบันได
chông ban dai

VOCABULARY

tiled floor
พื้นกระเบื้อง
péuun grà bêuang

carpet
พรม
prom

sofa bed
โซฟาเบด
soh faa bàyd

suite
ชุดรับแขก
chút ráp kàirk

armchair
โซฟาเดี่ยว
soh faa dìaw

footstool
ที่วางเท้า
têe waang táao

coffee table
โต๊ะกาแฟ
dtó gaa fair

ornament
ของตกแต่ง
kŏrng dtòk dtèng

wall light
ไฟผนัง
fai pà năng

table lamp
โคมไฟตั้งโต๊ะ
kohm fai dtâng dó

radio
วิทยุ
wít ta yú

DVD/Blu-ray® player
เครื่องเล่น ดีวีดี/
บลูเรย์
krêuang lên dee wee dee/
bloo ray

remote control
รีโมท
ree móht

to relax
พักผ่อน
pák porn

to watch TV
ดูทีวี
doo tee wee

YOU SHOULD KNOW...

Most lounges in Thai homes have wooden or tiled floors, rather than carpet.

GENERAL

bookcase
ชั้นวางหนังสือ
chán waang nang sěuu

curtains
ผ้าม่าน
pâa mâan

display cabinet
ตู้โชว์
dtôo choh

TV
ทีวี
tee wee

TV stand
ชั้นวางทีวี
chán waang tee wee

Venetian blind
มู่ลี่ปรับแสง
môo lêe bràp săirng

LOUNGE

picture
ภาพติดผนัง
pâap dtìt pà năng

cushion
หมอนอิง
mŏrn ing

wooden floor
พื้นไม้
péuun mái

sofa
โซฟา
soh faa

rug
พรม
prom

house plant
ต้นไม้ในบ้าน
dtôn máai nai bâan

Thai cooking is usually done on hobs and grills, and so most homes do not come equipped with Western-style ovens.

VOCABULARY

(electric) cooker	to boil	to steam
เตาไฟฟ้า	ต้ม	นึ่ง
dtao fai fáa	dtôm	nêung
gas cooker	to fry	to wash up
เตาแก๊ส	ทอด	ล้างจาน
dtao gáirt	tôrt	láang jaan
to cook	to stir-fry	to clean the worktops
ทำอาหาร	ผัด	เช็ด
tam aa hǎan	pàt	chét

YOU SHOULD KNOW...

Some apartments in the city do not come with any cooking facilities at all, but this is because there are usually a number of affordable takeaway options nearby.

MISCELLANEOUS ITEMS

aluminium foil
แผ่นฟอยล์
pèn foy

clingfilm
ฟิล์มถนอมอาหาร
fim tà nǒrm aa hǎan

kitchen roll
กระดาษ
อเนกประสงค์
grà dàat à nàyk bprà sǒng

chopping board
เขียง
kǐang

colander
กระชอน
grà chorn

cooker hood
เครื่องดูดควัน
krêuang dòot kwan

cooking pot
หม้อสองหู
môr sǒrng hǒo

electric rice cooker
หม้อหุงข้าวไฟฟ้า
môr hǔng kâao fai fáa

food processor
เครื่องหั่นอาหาร
krêuang hàn aa hǎan

frying pan
กระทะก้นแบน
grà tá gôn bairn

grater
ที่ขูดผัก
têe kòot pàk

kettle
กาต้มน้ำไฟฟ้า
gaa dtôm náam fai fáa

kitchen knife
มีดทำครัว
mêet tam krua

kitchen scales
เครื่องชั่งน้ำหนักในครัว
krêuang châng náam nàk
nai krua

ladle
ทัพพี
táp pee

measuring jug
ถ้วยตวง
tûay dtuang

pedal bin
ถังขยะแบบเหยียบ
tăng kà yà bàirp yìap

peeler
มีดปอกผลไม้
mêet bpòrk pŏn lá máai

pestle and mortar
ครก
krók

rolling pin
ไม้นวดแป้ง
máai nûat bpêng

saucepan
หม้อด้าม
môr dâam

sieve
ที่ร่อนแป้ง
têe rôrn bpêng

spatula
ตะหลิว
dtà lĭw

steamer
ซึ้งนึ่งซาลาเปา
sêung nêung saa laa bpao

teapot
กาน้ำชา
gaa nám chaa

tin opener
ที่เปิดกระป๋อง
têe bpèrt grà bpŏrng

toaster
เครื่องปิ้งขนมปัง
krêuang bpîng kà nŏm bpang

61

whisk
ตะกร้อมือ
dtà grôr meuu

wok
กระทะจีน
grà tá jeen

wooden spoon
ช้อนไม้
chórn máai

KITCHEN

sink
อ่างล้างจาน
àang láang jaan

oven
เตาอบ
dtao òp

hob
หัวเตา
hǔa dtao

microwave
ไมโครเวฟ
mai kroh wáyp

fridge-freezer
ตู้เย็น-ตู้แช่แข็ง
dtôo yen dtôo châir kěng

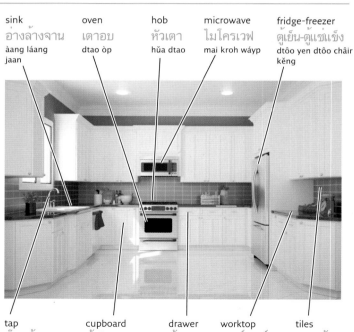

tap
ก๊อกน้ำ
górk náam

cupboard
ตู้เก็บของ
dtôo gèp kǒrng

drawer
ลิ้นชัก
lín chák

worktop
เคาท์เตอร์ครัว
kao dtêr krua

tiles
กระเบื้อง
grà bêuang

YOU MIGHT SAY/HEAR...

Enjoy your meal.
ทานให้อร่อยนะ
taan hâi à ròy ná

That was delicious!
อร่อยจัง!
à ròy jang

VOCABULARY

dining table	tablecloth	to dine
โต๊ะอาหาร	ผ้าปูโต๊ะ	ทานอาหาร
dtó aa hǎan	pâa bpoo dtó	taan aa hǎan
serving spoon	to set the table	to clear the table
ช้อนกลาง	จัดโต๊ะ	เช็ดโต๊ะ
chórn glaang	jàt dtó	chét dtó

YOU SHOULD KNOW...

Thai people usually eat using a spoon and fork. The fork is held in the left hand and the spoon in the right hand. The fork is used to push food onto the spoon, and the spoon to transport the food into the mouth.

When adopting European-style cutlery, Thais opted not to use knives, as this was seen as having a weapon at the dining table. What's more, Thai food tends to be cut into small pieces already, rendering a knife pointless. Some foods, including sticky rice, are still eaten using the fingers.

GENERAL

coffee cup
ถ้วยกาแฟ
tûay gaa fair

knife and fork
ส้อมกับมีด
sôm gàp mêet

mug
ถ้วยกาแฟ
tûay gaa fair

napkin
ผ้าเช็ดปาก
pâa chét bpàak

plate
จาน
jaan

spoon
ช้อน
chórn

teaspoon
ช้อนชา
chórn chaa

tumbler
แก้วน้ำทรงสูง
gâew náam song sŏong

wine glass
แก้วไวน์
gâew wai

TABLE SETTING

spoon and fork
ช้อนส้อม
chórn sôm

dinner plate
จานข้าว
jaan kâao

soup bowl
ถ้วยน้ำซุป
tûay náam súp

glass
แก้วน้ำ
gâew náam

VOCABULARY

single bed
เตียงเดี่ยว
dtiang dìaw

double bed
เตียงคู่
dtiang kôo

bunk beds
เตียงสองชั้น
dtiang sŏrng chán

master bedroom
ห้องนอนใหญ่
hông norn yài

spare room
ห้องว่าง
hông wâang

nursery
ห้องเด็กเล็ก
hông dèk lék

headboard
หัวเตียง
hŭa dtiang

to go to bed
ไปนอน
bpai norn

to sleep
นอน
norn

to wake up
ตื่น
dtèuun

to make the bed
จัดเตียง
jàt dtiang

to change the sheets
เปลี่ยนผ้าปูที่นอน
bplìan pâa bpoo têe norn

GENERAL

alarm clock
นาฬิกาปลุก
naa lí gaa bplùk

bedding
ชุดเครื่องนอน
chút krêuang norn

coat hanger
ไม้แขวนเสื้อ
máai kwăirn sêua

dressing table
โต๊ะเครื่องแป้ง
dtó krêuang bpêng

laundry basket
ตะกร้าผ้า
dtà grâa pâa

sheets
ผ้าปูที่นอน
pâa bpoo têe norn

65

mirror
กระจกเงา
grà jòk ngao

chest of drawers
ตู้ลิ้นชัก
dtôo lín chák

bed
เตียง
dtiang

wardrobe
ตู้เสื้อผ้า
dtôo sêua pâa

duvet
ผ้านวม
pâa nuam

curtains
ผ้าม่าน
pâa mâan

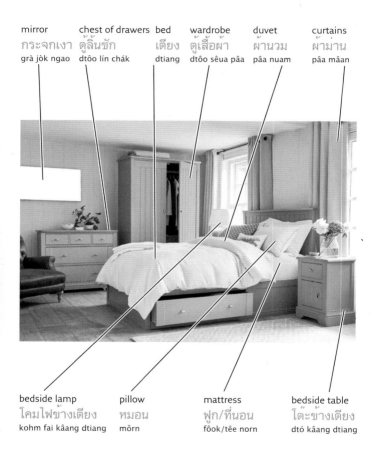

bedside lamp
โคมไฟข้างเตียง
kohm fai kâang dtiang

pillow
หมอน
mŏrn

mattress
ฟูก/ที่นอน
fôok/têe norn

bedside table
โต๊ะข้างเตียง
dtó kâang dtiang

66

As in the UK, most Thai homes have the toilet in the bathroom. Some homes in the countryside do not have Western-style showers or baths. Instead they have a water tank and scoop with which you can take a bucket bath by emptying the scoop over yourself. It is common to see a metal pressure hose with a nozzle next to the toilet. This performs a hygiene function similar to a French bidet.

VOCABULARY

shower curtain	to have a bath/shower	to brush one's teeth
ม่านห้องน้ำ	แช่น้ำ/อาบน้ำ	แปรงฟัน
mâan hông náam	châir náam/àap náam	bprairng fan
toiletries	to wash one's hands	to go to the toilet
ของใช้ในห้องน้ำ	ล้างมือ	ไปเข้าห้องน้ำ
kŏrng chái nai hông náam	láang meuu	bpai kâo hông náam

OTHER ITEMS

bath towel
ผ้าเช็ดตัว
pâa chét dtua

face cloth
ผ้าเช็ดหน้าขนหนู
pâa chét nâa kŏn nŏo

hairdryer
ไดร์เป่าผม
dai bpào pŏm

plastic slippers
รองเท้าแตะ
rorng táao dtè

shower puff
ใยขัดตัว
yai kàt dtua

soap
สบู่
sà bòo

sponge
ฟองน้ำ
forng náam

toilet brush
แปรงล้างห้องน้ำ
bprairng láang hông náam

toilet roll
กระดาษทิชชู่
grà dàat tít chôo

BATHROOM

mirror
กระจกเงา
grà jòk ngao

sink
อ่างล้างหน้า
àang láang nâa

shower
ฝักบัว
fàk bua

toilet
ชักโครก
chák krôhk

towel rail
ราวแขวนผ้า
raao kwǎirn pâa

tap
ก๊อกน้ำ
górk náam

cabinet
ตู้เก็บของ
dtôo gèp kŏrng

shower cubicle
ห้องอาบน้ำ
hông àap náam

bath
อ่างอาบน้ำ
àang àap náam

A lot of Thai apartments come with a balcony or roof space. This is often functional rather than for leisure purposes – the hot weather means that clothes are hung outside to dry.

VOCABULARY

flower	bird	to water
ดอกไม้	นก	รดน้ำต้นไม้
dòrk máai	nók	rót náam dtôn máai

weed	greenhouse	to grow
วัชพืช	กรีนเฮ้าส์	ปลูก
wát chá pêuut	green háo	bplòok

soil	to weed	to plant
ดิน	ถอนหญ้า	ปลูก
din	tŏrn yâa	bplòok

BALCONY

flowerpot stand	shrub	flowerpot	plant	decking
ชั้นวางกระถาง	ไม้พุ่ม	กระถาง	ต้นไม้	พื้นระเบียงไม้
chán waang grà tăang	máai pûm	grà tăang	dtôn máai	péuun rá biang máai

birdcage
กรงนก
grong nók

gardening gloves
ถุงมือทำสวน
tǔng meuu tam sǔan

trellis
ระแนงไม้เลื้อย
rá nairng máai léuay

trowel
ช้อนปลูก
chórn bplòok

watering can
บัวรดน้ำ
bua rót náam

weedkiller
ยาฆ่าหญ้า
yaa kâa yâa

windowbox
กระบะต้นไม้ริมหน้าต่าง
grà bà dtôn máai rim nâa dtàang

VOCABULARY

utility room
ห้องซักรีด
hông sák rêet

household appliances
เครื่องใช้ไฟฟ้า
krêuang chái fai fáa

dustbin
ถังขยะ
tăng kà yà

bleach
น้ำยาซักผ้าขาว
náam yaa sák pâa kăao

disinfectant
น้ำยาทำความ
สะอาดฆ่าเชื้อ
náam yaa tam kwaam sà
àat kâa chéua

washing-up liquid
น้ำยาล้างจาน
náam yaa láang jaan

to sweep the floor
กวาด
gwàat

to do the laundry
ซักผ้า
sák pâa

to hoover
ดูดฝุ่น
dòot fùn

to tidy up
จัดห้อง
jàt hông

to clean
ทำความสะอาด
tam kwaam sà àat

to take out the rubbish
เอาขยะไปทิ้ง
ao kà yà bpai tíng

bin bag
ถุงขยะ
tǔng kà yà

brush
แปรงถูพื้น
bprairng tŏo péuun

bucket
ถัง
tăng

cloth
ผ้าขนหนู
pâa kŏn nŏo

clothes horse
ราวตากผ้า
raao dtàk pâa

clothes pegs
ไม้หนีบผ้า
máai nèep pâa

dustpan
ที่โกยผง
têe gohy pǒng

iron
เตารีด
dtao rêet

ironing board
โต๊ะรีดผ้า
dtó rêet pâa

mop
ไม้ถูพื้น
máai tǒo péuun

rubber gloves
ถุงมือยาง
tǔng meuu yaang

scourer
ใยขัด
yai kàt

tumble drier
เครื่องอบผ้า
krêuang òp pâa

vacuum cleaner
เครื่องดูดฝุ่น
krêuang dòot fùn

washing line
เชือกตากผ้า
chêuak dtàk pâa

washing machine
เครื่องซักผ้า
krêuang sák pâa

washing powder
ผงซักฟอก
pǒng sák fôrk

wastepaper basket
ถังขยะตะแกรงเหล็ก
tǎng kà yà dtà grairng lèk

All over Thailand there are markets with delicious food and produce for sale. Markets are a popular place for tourists to pick up food, clothing, and souvenirs. Bangkok is also internationally famous for shopping, with a huge number of air-conditioned shopping centres selling a wide variety of different goods and catering to all budgets.

basket
ตะกร้า
dtà grâa

banana
กล้วย
glûay

bread
ขนมปัง
kà nŏm bpang

vegetable oil
น้ำมันพืช
nám man pêuut

Shops in Thailand are open 7 days a week until late in the evening; smaller corner shops may be open 24 hours a day in urban areas. Bangkok in particular has a huge number of air-conditioned convenience stores selling all kinds of essentials, drinks, and microwaveable ready meals which they will heat for you in the shop.

YOU MIGHT SAY...

Where is the nearest...?
ร้าน ... ที่ใกล้ที่สุดอยู่ที่ไหน
ráan ... têe glâi têe sùt yòo têe nǎi

Where can I buy...?
ผม/ฉัน ซื้อ ... ได้ที่ไหน
pǒm/chán séuu ... dâai têe nǎi

What time do you open/close?
เปิด/ปิด กี่โมง
bpèrt/bpìt gèe mohng

I'm just looking.
ผม/ฉัน ขอดูก่อน
pǒm/chán kǒr doo gòrn

Do you sell...?
คุณขาย ... ไหม
kun kǎai ... mái

Can I pay by cash/card?
ผม/ฉัน จ่ายด้วย เงินสด/บัตร ได้ไหม
pǒm/chán jàai dûay nguhn sòt/bàt dâai mái

Can I pay with my mobile app?
ผม/ฉัน จ่ายด้วยแอปมือถือได้ไหม
pǒm/chán jàai dûay èp meuu těuu dâai mái

How much does this cost?
นี่ราคาเท่าไหร่
nêe raa kaa tâo rài

How much is delivery?
ค่าส่งเท่าไหร่
kâa sòng tâo rài

I need/would like...
ผม/ฉัน ต้องการ/อยากได้...
pǒm/chán dtông gaan/yàak dâai...

Can I exchange this?
ผม/ฉัน ขอเปลี่ยนของได้ไหม
pǒm/chán kǒr bplìan kǒrng dâai mái

Can I get a refund?
ผม/ฉัน ขอเงินคืนได้ไหม
pǒm/chán kǒr nguhn keuun dâai mái

Can you recommend...?
คุณช่วยแนะนำ ... ได้ไหม
kun chûay né nam ... dâai mái

That's all, thank you.
เท่านั้น ครับ/ค่ะ ขอบคุณ
tâo nán kráp/kâ kòrp kun

Can I help you?
ให้ช่วยอะไรไหม ครับ/คะ
hâi chûay à rai mái kráp/ká

Are you looking for anything in particular?
หาอะไรเป็นพิเศษรึเปล่า ครับ/คะ
hăa à rai bpen pí sàyt réu bplàao kráp/ká

I would recommend...
ผม/ฉัน ขอแนะนำ...
pŏm/chán kŏr né nam...

Would you like anything else?
รับอะไรเพิ่มอีกไหม
ráp à rai pêrm èek mái

It costs...
ราคา...
raa kaa...

I'm sorry, we don't have...
ขอโทษ ครับ/คะ เราไม่มี...
kŏr tôht kráp/kâ rao mâi mee...

I can order that for you.
ผม/ฉัน สั่งของให้คุณได้
pŏm/chán sàng kŏrng hâi kun dâai

How would you like to pay?
คุณจะจ่ายยังไง ครับ/คะ
kun jà jàai yang ngai kráp/ká

Can you enter your PIN?
ช่วยกดรหัสได้ไหม ครับ/คะ
chûay gòt rá hàt dâai mái kráp/ká

Would you like a receipt?
รับใบเสร็จไหม ครับ/คะ
ráp bai sèt mái kráp/ká

Have you got a receipt?
มีใบเสร็จไหม
mee bai sèt mái

We'd love to see you again soon.
ไว้มาอีกนะ ครับ/คะ
wái maa èek ná kráp/ká

VOCABULARY

shop
ร้าน
ráan

supermarket
ซุปเปอร์มาร์เก็ต
súp bper maa gèt

corner shop
ร้านหัวมุม
ráan hŭa mum

shopping centre
ศูนย์การค้า
sŏon gaan káa

market
ตลาด
dtà làat

cash
เงินสด
nguhn sòt

change
เงินทอน
nguhn torn

PIN
รหัส
rá hàt

checkout
จุดจ่ายเงิน
jùt jàai nguhn

exchange	voucher	to buy
แลกเปลี่ยน	บัตรแทนเงินสด	ซื้อ
lâirk bplìan	bàt tairn nguhn sòt	séuu

refund	gift voucher	to pay
ขอเงินคืน	บัตรกำนัล	จ่าย
kŏr nguhn keuun	bàt gam nan	jàai

receipt	to browse	to shop (online)
ใบเสร็จรับเงิน	ดูเฉยๆ	ซื้อของ (ออนไลน์)
bai sèt ráp nguhn	doo chŏey chŏey	séuu kŏrng (orn lai)

YOU SHOULD KNOW...

Thanks to growing public awareness about the risks to the natural environment, Thailand has started to introduce tough measures to reduce the amount of plastic waste being produced. This includes banning certain retailers from offering plastic bags altogether.

banknotes
แบงค์/ธนบัตร
béng/tá ná bàt

card reader
เครื่องอ่านบัตร
krêuang àan bàt

coins
เหรียญ
rĭan

debit/credit card
บัตร เดบิต/เครดิต
bàt day bìt/kray dìt

paper bag
ถุงกระดาษ
tŭng grà dàat

plastic bag
ถุงพลาสติก
tŭng pláat dtìk

SUPERMARKET | ซุปเปอร์มาร์เก็ต

Many Thai supermarkets offer online shopping and delivery services. Due to the increasingly strict measures intended to curb plastic bag use, you should remember to bring your own bags for your shopping.

YOU MIGHT SAY...

Where can I find...?
ผม/ฉัน จะซื้อ ... ได้ที่ไหน
pǒm/chán jà séuu ... dâai têe nǎi

I'm looking for...
ผม/ฉัน หา...
pǒm/chán hǎa...

Do you have...?
มี ... ไหม
mee ... mái

Do you have carrier bags?
มีถุงไหม
mee tǔng mái

YOU MIGHT HEAR...

We have/don't have...
มี/ไม่มี...
mee/mâi mee...

I can show you.
หาของให้ดูได้ ครับ/ค่ะ
hǎa kǒrng hâi doo dâai kráp/kâ

It's in aisle 1/2/3.
อยู่ที่แถว 1/2/3
yòo têe tǎew nèung/sǒrng/sǎam

There is a charge for a carrier bag.
คิดเงินค่าถุง
kít nguhn kâa tǔng

VOCABULARY

shop assistant
พนักงานขาย
pá nák ngaan kǎai

aisle
แถว
tǎew

groceries
ของกินของใช้
kǒrng gin kǒrng chái

ready meal
อาหารพร้อม
รับประทาน
aa hǎan prórm
ráp bprà taan

bottle
ขวด
kùat

box
กล่อง
glòrng

carton
กล่องกระดาษ
glòrng grà dàat

jar
ขวดโหล
kùat lǒh

multipack	tinned	dairy
แพ็คหลายชิ้น	กระป๋อง	ผลิตภัณฑ์นม
pék lăai chín	grà bpŏrng	pà lìt dtà pan nom

packet	fresh	low-fat
ห่อ	สด	ไขมันต่ำ
hòr	sòt	kăi man dtàm

tin	frozen	low-calorie
กระป๋อง	แช่แข็ง	แคลอรี่ต่ำ
grà bpŏrng	châir kĕng	kair lor rêe dtàm

GENERAL

basket
ตะกร้า
dtà grâa

scales
ตาชั่ง
dtaa châng

trolley
รถเข็น
rót kĕn

GROCERIES

biscuits
คุกกี้
kúk gêe

honey
น้ำผึ้ง
nám pêung

instant coffee
กาแฟสำเร็จรูป
gaa fair săm rèt rôop

jam
แยม
yairm

ketchup
ซอสมะเขือเทศ
sórt má kĕua tâyt

noodles
เส้นก๋วยเตี๋ยว
sên gŭay dtĭaw

olive oil
น้ำมันมะกอก
nám man má gòrk

pepper
พริกไทย
prík tai

rice
ข้าวสาร
kâao săan

salt
เกลือ
gleua

soy sauce
ซอสถั่วเหลือง
sórt tùa lĕuang

sugar
น้ำตาล
nám dtaan

teabags
ชาในถุง
chaa nai tŭng

vegetable oil
น้ำมันพืช
nám man pêuut

vinegar
น้ำส้มสายชู
nám sôm săai choo

79

SNACKS

chocolate
ช็อกโกแลต
chók go lét

crisps
มันฝรั่งทอดกรอบ
man fà ràng tôrt gròrp

dried fruit
ผลไม้อบแห้ง
pǒn lá máai òp hâirng

nuts
ถั่ว
tùa

popcorn
ข้าวโพดคั่ว
kâao pôht kûa

sweets
ลูกอม
lôok om

DRINKS

beer
เบียร์
bia

fizzy drink
น้ำอัดลม
náam àt lom

fruit juice
น้ำผลไม้
náam pǒn lá máai

spirits
เหล้า
lâo

still water
น้ำดื่ม
náam dèuum

wine
ไวน์
wai

MARKET | ตลาด

Local markets are an important part of daily life for many Thais all over the country. Some markets are more geared towards tourists than others, and some of the more modern, trendy markets sell various kinds of handicrafts.

YOU MIGHT SAY...

Do you have...?
มี ... ไหม
mee ... mái

Where is the market?
ตลาดอยู่ที่ไหน
dtà làat yòo têe nǎi

500 grams/A kilo of...
... ครึ่งกิโล/หนึ่งกิโล
... krêung gì loh/nèung gì loh

Two/Three ..., please.
สอง/สาม ... ครับ/ค่ะ
sǒrng/sǎam ... kráp/kâ

A slice of ..., please.
... หนึ่งชิ้น ครับ/ค่ะ
... nèung chín kráp/kâ

What do I owe you?
ทั้งหมดเท่าไหร่
táng mòt tâo rài

YOU MIGHT HEAR...

The market is in the square.
มีตลาดที่ลาน
mee dtà làat têe laan

What would you like?
เอาอะไร
ao à rai

That will be...
... บาท
... bàat

There is no more...
... หมดแล้ว
... mòt láew

Here you go. Anything else?
นี่ ครับ/ค่ะ รับอะไรอีกไหม
nêe kráp/kâ ráp à rai èek mái

Here's your change.
นี่เงินทอน ครับ/ค่ะ
nêe nguhn torn kráp/kâ

YOU SHOULD KNOW...

Traditional Thai-style "floating markets" are often found on canals. Some of these may be modern reconstructions but they remain popular with local and foreign tourists.

81

indoor market	local	seasonal
ตลาดในร่ม	ท้องถิ่น	ตามฤดูกาล
dtà làat nai rôm	tórng tìn	dtaam réu doo gaan

night market	organic	home-made
ตลาดกลางคืน	ออร์แกนิก	โฮม-เมด
dtà làat glaang keuun	or gair ník	hohm màyt

YOU SHOULD KNOW...

It is normal to haggle over goods in markets, particularly for non-edibles or things without price tags. However, Thai vendors tend not to set the prices too high in the first place so it is not normally necessary to bargain hard.

MARKETPLACE

trader	stall	customers
คนขาย	แผง	ลูกค้า
kon kǎai	pǎirng	lôok káa

basket	plastic bag	produce	crate
ตะกร้า	ถุงพลาสติก	ผักผลไม้สด	ลัง
dtà grâa	tǔng pláat dtìk	pàk pǒn lá máai sòt	lang

FRUIT AND VEGETABLES | ผักและผลไม้

YOU MIGHT SAY...

Where can I buy...?
ซื้อ ... ได้ที่ไหน
séuu ... dâai têe năi

Can I have...?
เอา ... นะ ครับ/คะ
ao ... ná kráp/ká

Are they ripe/fresh?
สุก/สด ไหม
sùk/sòt mái

YOU MIGHT HEAR...

What would you like?
เอาอะไร
ao à rai

I'm sorry, we don't have...
ขอโทษ ครับ/ค่ะ เราไม่มี...
kŏr tôht kráp/kâ rao mâi mee...

They are ripe/fresh.
สุก/สด
sùk/sòt

VOCABULARY

grocer's ร้านของชำ ráan kŏrng cham	pip/seed เมล็ด má lét	fresh สด sòt
root vegetable ผักกินหัว pàk gin hŭa	segment ชิ้น chín	rotten เน่า nâo
juice น้ำผักผลไม้ náam pàk pŏn lá mái	core แกน gairn	ripe สุก sùk
leaf ใบ bai	stone เมล็ด má lét	unripe ยังไม่สุก yang mâi sùk
peel/rind/skin เปลือก bplèuak	raw ดิบ dìp	seedless ไร้เมล็ด rái má lét

to chop	to grate	to peel
หั่น	ขูด	ปอก
hàn	kòot	bpòrk

to dice	to juice	to wash
หั่นเป็นชิ้นลูกเต๋า	คั้น	ล้าง
hàn bpen chín lôok dtăo	kán	láang

When specifying weights, it is common to ask for things in "kèet" (ขีด). This word literally means "line", referring to the lines on weighing scales representing increments of 100 grams. Thus if you want to ask for 300 grams, you could say "3 kèet".

FRUIT

banana
กล้วย
glûay

cantaloupe
แคนตาลูป
kairn dtaa lóop

coconut
มะพร้าว
má práao

durian
ทุเรียน
tú rian

grape
องุ่น
à ngùn

guava
ฝรั่ง
fà ràng

jackfruit
ขนุน
kà nǔn

jujube
พุทรา
pút saa

lemon
เลมอน
lay morn

longan
ลำไย
lam yai

lychee
ลิ้นจี่
lín jèe

mango
มะม่วง
má mûang

mangosteen
มังคุด
mang kút

mulberry
ลูกหม่อน
lôok mòrn

orange
ส้ม
sôm

passion fruit
เสาวรส
sǎo wá rót

persimmon
พลับ
pláp

pineapple
สับปะรด
sàp bpà rót

pomegranate
ทับทิม
táp tim

pomelo
ส้มโอ
sôm oh

rambutan
เงาะ
ngó

rose apple
ชมพู่
chom pôo

strawberry
สตรอเบอรี่
sà dtror ber rêe

watermelon
แตงโม
dtairng moh

VEGETABLES

asparagus
หน่อไม้ฝรั่ง
nòr máai fà ràng

aubergine
มะเขือม่วง
má kěua mûang

bamboo shoots
หน่อไม้
nòr máai

broccoli
บร็อคโคลี่
bròk koh lêe

cabbage
กะหล่ำปลี
gà làm bplee

carrot
แครอท
kair ròt

cauliflower
ดอกกะหล่ำ
dòrk gà làm

celery
ขึ้นฉ่ายฝรั่ง
kêun chàai fà ràng

chilli
พริก
prík

Chinese broccoli
คะน้า
ká náa

Chinese cabbage
ผักกาดขาว
pàk gàat kǎao

cucumber
แตงกวา
dtairng gwaa

garlic
กระเทียม
grà tiam

green beans
ถั่วแขก
tùa kàirk

lettuce
ผักกาดแก้ว
pàk gàat gâew

mushroom
เห็ด
hèt

onion
หอมใหญ่
hǒrm yài

pak choi
ผักฮ่องเต้
pàk hông dtây

peas
ถั่วลันเตา
tùa lón dtao

potato
มันฝรั่ง
man fà ràng

red pepper
พริกหวาน
prík wăn

spinach
ผักโขม
pàk kŏhm

spring onion
ต้นหอม
dtôn hŏrm

Thai basil
ใบโหระพา
bai hŏh rá paa

water spinach
ผักบุ้ง
pàk bûng

tomato
มะเขือเทศ
má kĕua tâyt

winter melon
ฟักเขียว
fák kĭaw

Ask the fishmonger for tips on what is fresh, what has been frozen, and what is in season.

YOU MIGHT SAY...

How fresh is this fish?
ปลานี้สดไหม
bplaa née sòt mái

I'd like the scales removed, please.
ช่วยขอดเกล็ดให้หน่อย ครับ/
ค่ะ
chûay kòrt glèt hâi nòy kráp/kâ

Are there a lot of bones in this fish?
ปลานี้ก้างเยอะไหม
bplaa née gâang yúh mái

YOU MIGHT HEAR...

This fish was caught in the river this morning.
ปลาตกจากแม่น้ำเข้านี้เอง
bplaa dtòk jàak mâir náam cháao née ayng

Would you like the scales/guts removed?
ให้ ขอดเกล็ด/ล้างปลา ไหม
ครับ/คะ
hâi kòrt glèt/láang bplaa mái kráp/ká

VOCABULARY

fishmonger ร้านขายปลา ráan kăai bplaa	shell เปลือก bplèuak	farmed เลี้ยง líang
shellfish หอย hŏy	roe ไข่ kài	wild ธรรมชาติ tam má châat
scales เกล็ด glèt	freshwater น้ำจืด náam jèuut	salted เค็ม kem
bone ก้าง gâang	saltwater น้ำเค็ม náam kem	smoked รมควัน rom kwan

anchovy
แอนโชวี
airn choh wee

carp
ปลาตะเพียน
bplaa dtà pian

catfish
ปลาดุก
bplaa dùk

grouper
ปลาเก๋า
bplaa gǎo

mackerel
ปลาทู
bplaa too

Nile tilapia
ปลานิล
bplaa nin

salmon
ปลาแซลมอน
bplaa sair môn

sardine
ปลาซาร์ดีน
bplaa saa deen

sea bass
ปลากะพง
bplaa gà pong

snakehead
ปลาช่อน
bplaa chôn

tuna
ปลาทูน่า
bplaa too nâa

white pomfret
ปลาจะละเม็ดขาว
bplaa jà lá mét kǎao

clam
หอยลาย
hŏy laai

crab
ปู
bpoo

crayfish
กุ้งเครย์ฟิช
gûng kray fít

lobster
กุ้งล็อบสเตอร์
gûng lóp sà dtěr

mussel
หอยแมลงภู่
hŏy má lairng pôo

octopus
หมึกสาย
mèuk săai

oyster
หอยนางรม
hŏy naang rom

prawn
กุ้ง
gûng

scallop
หอยเชลล์
hŏy chayn

sea urchin
เม่นทะเล
mâyn tá lay

shrimp
กุ้ง
gûng

squid
หมึก
mèuk

Butchers in Thailand are often able to recommend what kind of cuts to buy for the recipes you'd like to try, as well as local specialities they may sell.

YOU MIGHT SAY...

A kilo of...
... หนึ่งกิโล
... nèung gì loh

Can you slice this for me, please?
ช่วยหั่นให้หน่อยได้ไหม ครับ/คะ
chûay hàn hâi nòy dâai mái kráp/ká

Can you remove the bone for me, please?
ช่วยเลาะกระดูกให้หน่อย ครับ/คะ
chûay ló grà dòok hâi nòy kráp/ká

YOU MIGHT HEAR...

Certainly, sir/madam.
ได้เลย ครับ/คะ
dâai loey kráp/kâ

How much/many would you like?
เอาเยอะไหม ครับ/คะ
ao yúh mái kráp/ká

Will 2 pieces/half a kilo be enough?
2 ชิ้น/ครึ่งโล พอไหม ครับ/คะ
sŏrng chín/krêung loh por mái kráp/ká

VOCABULARY

butcher
คนขายเนื้อ
kon kăai néua

meat
เนื้อสัตว์
néua sàt

red/white meat
เนื้อ แดง/ขาว
néua dairng/kăao

cold meats
แฮมชนิดต่างๆ
hairm chá nít dtàang dtàang

pork
หมู
mŏo

beef
เนื้อวัว
néua wua

lamb
เนื้อแกะ
néua gè

game
สัตว์ป่า
sàt bpàa

venison
เนื้อกวาง
néua gwaang

offal
เครื่องใน
krêuang nai

poultry
สัตว์ปีก
sàt bpèek

chicken
ไก่
gài

duck เป็ด bpèt	raw ดิบ dìp	organic ออร์แกนิก or gair ník
goose ห่าน hàan	cooked ปรุงสุก bprung sùk	free-range เลี้ยงแบบปล่อย líang bàirp bplòy

bacon
เบคอน
bay korn

beefburger
เบอร์เกอร์เนื้อ
ber ger néua

cured sausage
ไส้กรอกอบแห้ง
sâi gròrk òp hâirng

ham
แฮม
hairm

joint
เนื้อสำหรับอบ
néua săm ràp òp

mince
เนื้อ/หมู บด
néua/mŏo bòt

ribs
ซี่โครง
sêe krohng

sausage
ไส้กรอก
sâi gròrk

steak
สเต๊ก
sà dtáyk

Bakeries are now fairly commonplace in Thailand. Some of them also have seating areas and serve coffees and teas. In some shopping centres you can find bakeries or speciality supermarkets selling European-style baked goods.

YOU MIGHT SAY...

Where is the...?
... อยู่ที่ไหน
... yòo têe nǎi

What time do you open/close?
เปิด/ปิด กี่โมง
bpèrt/bpìt gèe mòhng

Do you sell...?
คุณมี ... ไหม
kun mee ... mái

May I have...?
ขอ ... ได้ไหม ครับ/คะ
kǒr ... dâai mái kráp/ká

YOU MIGHT HEAR...

Are you being served?
สั่งรึยัง ครับ/คะ
sàng réu yang kráp/ká

Would you like anything else?
รับอะไรเพิ่มอีกไหม ครับ/คะ
ráp à rai pêrm èek mái kráp/ká

It costs...
ราคา ... บาท
raa kaa ... bàat

I'm sorry, we don't have...
ขอโทษ ครับ/ค่ะ เราไม่มี...
kǒr tôht kráp/kâ rao mâi mee...

VOCABULARY

baker	dough	slice
คนอบขนม	แป้งดิบ	ชิ้น
kon òp kà nǒm	bpêng dìp	chín
bread	flour	gluten-free
ขนมปัง	แป้ง	ไม่ใส่กลูเต็น
kà nǒm bpang	bpêng	mâi sài gloo dten
loaf	steamed bun	to bake
แถว	ซาลาเปา	อบ
tǎew	saa laa bpao	òp

baguette
ขนมปังฝรั่งเศส
kà nŏm bpang fà ràng sàyt

bread rolls
ขนมปังก้อน
kà nŏm bpang gôn

croissant
ครัวซ็อง
krua song

Danish pastry
เดนิช
day nít

doughnut
โดนัท
doh nát

éclair
เอแคลร์
ay klair

fruit tart
ทาร์ตผลไม้
táat pŏn la máai

macaroon
มาการง
maa gaa rong

pain au chocolat
ครัวซ็องช็อกโกแลต
krua song chók goh lét

pancakes
แพนเค้ก
pairn káyk

waffle
วาฟเฟิล
wáap fêrn

wholemeal bread
ขนมปังสีน้ำตาล
kà nŏm bpang sĕe nám
dtaan

95

Fresh milk and yoghurt products are widely available in local convenience stores. European-style cheese is less popular but is available in supermarkets.

VOCABULARY

egg white/yolk
ไข่ขาว/ไข่แดง
kài kăao/kài dairng

cheese
ชีส
chéet

pasteurized/
unpasteurized
พาสเจอร์ไรส์/
ไม่พาสเจอร์ไรส์
páat jer rái/mâi páat jer rái

UHT milk
นมยูเอชที
nom yoo àyt tee

caged
ในกรง
nai grong

fresh milk
นมสด
nom sòt

free-range
เลี้ยงแบบปล่อย
líang bàirp bplòy

dairy-free
ไม่ใส่ผลิตภัณฑ์นม
mâi sài pà lìt dtà pan nom

butter
เนย
noey

cream
ครีม
kreem

egg
ไข่
kài

milk
นม
nom

soymilk
นมถั่วเหลือง
nom tùa lĕuang

yoghurt
โยเกิร์ต
yoh gèrt

Pharmacies are easy to find and tend to be well stocked with common medicines and treatments like paracetamol or antiseptic solution.

YOU MIGHT SAY...

I need something for...
ผม/ฉัน อยากได้ยาสำหรับ...
pǒm/chán yàak dâai yaa sǎm ràp...

I'm allergic to...
ผม/ฉัน แพ้ยา...
pǒm/chán páir yaa...

What would you recommend?
คุณแนะนำยาอะไร
kun né nam yaa à rai

Is it suitable for young children?
ยานี้เด็กใช้ได้ไหม
yaa née dèk chái dâai mái

YOU MIGHT HEAR...

Do you have a prescription?
คุณมีใบสั่งยาไหม
kun mee bai sàng yaa mái

Do you have ID?
คุณมีบัตรประจำตัวไหม
kun mee bàt bprà jam dtua mái

Do you have any allergies?
คุณแพ้ยาอะไรไหม
kun páir yaa à rai mái

Take two tablets twice a day.
กินครั้งละสองเม็ด วันละสองครั้ง
gin kráng lá sǒrng mét, wan lá sǒrng kráng

You should see a doctor.
คุณควรไปหาหมอ
kun kuan bpai hǎa mǒr

You need a prescription to buy that.
ต้องมีใบสั่งยาถึงจะซื้อได้
dtông mee bai sàng yaa tĕung jà séuu dâai

I'd recommend...
ผม/ฉัน แนะนำให้ใช้...
pǒm/chán né nam hâi chái...

VOCABULARY

pharmacist	cabinet	counter
เภสัชกร	ตู้ยา	เคาน์เตอร์
pay sàt chá gorn	dtôo yaa	kao dtêr

prescription
ใบสั่งยา
bai sàng yaa

painkiller
ยาแก้ปวด
yaa gâir bpùat

hay fever
แพ้ละอองเกสร
páir lá orng gay sŏrn

antihistamine
ยาแก้แพ้
yaa gâir páir

flu tablets
ยาแก้หวัด
yaa gâir wàt

headache
ปวดหัว
bpùat hŭa

antiseptic
ยาฆ่าเชื้อ
yaa kâa chéua

diarrhoea tablets
ยาแก้ท้องเสีย
yaa gâir tórng sĭa

sore throat
เจ็บคอ
jèp kor

decongestant
แก้คัดจมูก
gâir kát jà mòok

tube
หลอด
lòrt

flu
ไข้หวัด
kâi wàt

medicine
ยา
yaa

cold
ไข้หวัด
kâi wàt

stomachache
ปวดท้อง
bpùat tórng

ointment
ยาขี้ผึ้ง
yaa kêe pêung

diarrhoea
ท้องเสีย
tórng sĭa

asthma
หอบหืด
hòrp hèuut

Hygiene and beauty items are not available in pharmacies in Thailand, but are sold in beauty shops.

GENERAL

antiseptic cream
ครีมฆ่าเชื้อโรค
kreem kâa chéua rôhk

bandage
ผ้าพันแผล
pâa pan plăir

capsule
แคปซูล
káirp soon

condom
ถุงยางอนามัย
tǔng yaang à naa mai

cough mixture
ยาน้ำแก้ไอ
yaa náam gâir ai

drops
หยด
yòt

insect repellent
ยากันแมลง
yaa gan má lairng

lozenge
ยาอมแก้ไอ
yaa om gâir ai

plaster
พลาสเตอร์
pláat dtêr

sun cream
ครีมกันแดด
kreem gan dàirt

protective face mask
หน้ากากกันฝุ่น
nâa gàak gan fùn

tablet/pill
ยาเม็ด
yaa mét

HYGIENE

antiperspirant
ยาระงับเหงื่อ
yaa rá ngáp ngèua

conditioner
ครีมนวดผม
kreem nûat pǒm

mouthwash
น้ำยาบ้วนปาก
nám yaa bûan bpàak

razor
มีดโกนหนวด
mêet gohn nùat

sanitary towel
ผ้าอนามัย
pâa à naa mai

shampoo
แชมพู
chairm poo

shaving foam
ครีมโกนหนวด
kreem gohn nùat

shower gel
เจลอาบน้ำ
jayw àap náam

soap
สบู่
sà bòo

tampon
ผ้าอนามัยแบบสอด
pâa à naa mai bàirp sòrt

toothbrush
แปรงสีฟัน
bprairng sěe fan

toothpaste
ยาสีฟัน
yaa sěe fan

blusher
ปัดแก้ม
bpàt gâirm

comb
หวี
wěe

eyeliner
อายไลเนอร์
aai lai nêr

eyeshadow
สีแต่งตา
sěe dtèng dtaa

foundation
รองพื้น
rorng péuun

hairbrush
แปรงผม
bprairng pŏm

hairspray
สเปรย์ฉีดผม
sà bpray chèet pŏm

lip balm
ลิปบาล์ม
líp baam

lipstick
ลิปสติก
líp sà dtìk

mascara
มาสคารา
máat kaa raa

nail varnish
สีทาเล็บ
sěe taa lép

powder
แป้ง
bpâirng

VOCABULARY

nappy rash
ผื่นผ้าอ้อม
pèuun pâa ôrm

dummy
จุกนมหลอก
juk nom lòrk

to breast-feed
ให้นมลูก
hâi nom lôok

baby lotion
โลชั่นสำหรับเด็ก
loh chân săm ràp dèk

to be teething
ฟันขึ้น
fan kêun

CLOTHING

babygro®/sleepsuit
ชุดหมีของเด็ก
chút mĕe kŏrng dèk

bib
ผ้ากันเปื้อนเด็ก
pâa gan bpêuan dèk

bootees
รองเท้าเด็กอ่อน
rorng táao dèk òrn

hat
หมวกเด็ก
mùak dèk

mittens
ถุงมือเด็กอ่อน
tŭng meuu dèk òrn

vest
บอดี้สูทเด็ก
bor dêe sòot dèk

HEALTH AND HYGIENE

baby food
อาหารเด็ก
aa hăan dèk

baby's bottle
ขวดนม
kùat nom

changing bag
กระเป๋าผ้าอ้อม
grà bpăo pâa ôrm

cotton bud
ค็อตตอนบัด
kót dtorn bàt

cotton wool
สำลีก้อน
săm lee gôrn

formula milk
นมผงสำหรับเด็ก
nom pŏng săm ràp dèk

nappy
ผ้าอ้อม
pâa ôrm

nappy cream
ครีมทาพื้นผ้าอ้อม
kreem taa pèuun pâa ôrm

wet wipes
ทิชชูเปียก
tít chôo bpìak

ACCESSORIES

baby bath
อ่างอาบน้ำเด็ก
àang àap náam dèk

baby sling
ผ้าอุ้มเด็ก
pâa ûm dèk

cot
เปล
bplay

highchair
เก้าอี้เด็ก
gâo êe dèk

pram
รถเข็นเด็ก
rót kĕn dèk

pushchair
รถเข็นเด็ก
rót kĕn dèk

ร้านหนังสือพิมพ์และร้านสะดวกซื้อ

Urban areas in Thailand have a large number of convenience stores which stock a wide range of food, stationery, alcohol, tobacco, and hygiene products. Many will also sell newspapers, magazines, comics, and novels but, like elsewhere in the world, demand for these is being affected by technological advances.

VOCABULARY

kiosk ตู้ขายของอัตโนมัติ dtôo kăai kŏrng àt dtà noh mát	tobacconist คนขายบุหรี่ kon kăai bù rèe	daily รายวัน raai wan
stationery เครื่องเขียน krêuang kĭan	vendor คนขาย kon kăai	weekly รายสัปดาห์ raai sàp daa

book
หนังสือ
nang sĕuu

cigarette
บุหรี่
bù rèe

comic book
หนังสือการ์ตูน
nang sĕuu gaa dtoon

confectionery
ลูกอม
lôok om

envelope
ซองจดหมาย
sorng jòt măai

greetings card
การ์ดอวยพร
gàat uay porn

lottery ticket
ล็อตเตอรี่
lót dter rêe

magazine
นิตยสาร
nít dtà yà săan

map
แผนที่
păirn têe

newspaper
หนังสือพิมพ์
nang sĕuu pim

notebook
สมุด
sà mùt

pen
ปากกา
bpàak gaa

pencil
ดินสอ
din sŏr

postcard
โปสการ์ด
bpòht gàat

stamp
แสตมป์
sà dtáirm

YOU MIGHT SAY...

Where is...?
... อยู่ที่ไหน
... yòo têe nǎi

Which floor is this?
นี่ชั้นอะไร
nêe chán à rai

Can you gift-wrap this, please?
ช่วยห่อของขวัญได้ไหม
chûay hòr kǒrng kwǎn dâai mái

YOU MIGHT HEAR...

Menswear is on the second floor.
เสื้อผ้าผู้ชายอยู่ชั้นสอง
sêua pâa pôo chaai yòo chán sǒrng

This is the first floor.
ที่นี่ชั้นหนึ่ง
têe nêe chán nèung

Would you like this gift-wrapped?
ห่อของขวัญไหม ครับ/คะ
hòr kǒrng kwǎn mái kráp/ká

VOCABULARY

floor
ชั้น
chán

counter
เคาน์เตอร์
kao dtêr

sportswear
ชุดกีฬา
chút gee laa

escalator
บันไดเลื่อน
ban dai lêuan

department
แผนก
pà nàirk

swimwear
ชุดว่ายน้ำ
chút wâai náam

lift
ลิฟต์
líp

menswear
เสื้อผ้าผู้ชาย
sêua pâa pôo chaai

brand
ยี่ห้อ
yêe hôr

toilets
ห้องน้ำ
hông náam

womenswear
เสื้อผ้าผู้หญิง
sêua pâa pôo yǐng

sale
ลดราคา
lót raa kaa

YOU SHOULD KNOW...

Note that the ground floor in the UK is the first floor in Thailand; the first floor in the UK is the second floor in Thailand, and so on. However, there are certain malls and large buildings that do not follow this convention.

accessories
เครื่องประดับ
krêuang bprà dàp

cosmetics
เครื่องสำอาง
krêuang săm aang

fashion
แฟชั่น
fair chân

food and drink
อาหารและเครื่องดื่ม
aa hăan lé krêuang dèuum

footwear
รองเท้า
rorng táao

furniture
เฟอร์นิเจอร์
fer ní jêr

kitchenware
เครื่องครัว
krêuang krua

leather goods
เครื่องหนัง
krêuang năng

lighting
โคมไฟตกแต่ง
kohm fai dtòk dtèng

lingerie
ชั้นในสตรี
chán nai sà dtree

soft furnishings
ผ้าตกแต่งบ้าน
pâa dtòk dtèng bâan

toys
ของเล่น
kŏrng lên

YOU MIGHT SAY...

I'm just looking.
ผม/ฉัน กำลังหา...
pǒm/chán gam lang hǎa ...

I'd like to try this on, please.
ขอลองใส่ได้ไหม ครับ/คะ
kǒr lorng sài dâai mái kráp/ká

Where are the fitting rooms?
ห้องลองอยู่ไหน
hông lorng yòo nǎi

I'm a size...
ผม/ฉัน ใส่ไซส์...
pǒm/chán sài sái...

Have you got a bigger/smaller size?
มีไซส์ ใหญ่กว่า/เล็กกว่า นี้ไหม
mee sái yài gwàa/lék gwàa née mái

This is too small/big.
นี่ เล็ก/ใหญ่ เกินไป
nêe lék/yài gern bpai

This is too tight/short/long.
นี่ คับ/สั้น/ยาว เกินไป
nêe káp/sân/yaao gern bpai

This is torn.
มีรอยขาด
mee roy kàat

It's not my style.
มันไม่ใช่สไตล์ของ ผม/ฉัน
man mâi châi sà dtai kǒrng pǒm/chán

YOU MIGHT HEAR...

Can I help you?
ให้ช่วยอะไรไหม ครับ/คะ
hâi chûay à rai mái kráp/ká

Let me know if I can help.
ให้ช่วยอะไรบอกนะ ครับ/คะ
hâi chûay à rai bòrk ná kráp/ká

The fitting rooms are over there.
ห้องลองอยู่ทางนั้น
hông lorng yòo taang nán

What (dress) size are you?
คุณใส่ (ชุด) ไซส์อะไร
kun sài (chút) sái à rai

What shoe size are you?
คุณใส่รองเท้าเบอร์อะไร
kun sài rorng táao ber à rai

I'm sorry, it's out of stock.
ขอโทษ ครับ/ค่ะ ของหมดแล้ว
kǒr tôht kráp/kâ kǒrng mòt láew

I'm sorry, we don't have that size/colour.
ขอโทษ ครับ/ค่ะ เราไม่มี ไซส์/สี นั้น
kǒr tôht kráp/kâ rao mâi mee sái/sěe nán

That suits you.
เหมาะกับคุณ
mò gàp kun

VOCABULARY

fitting room
ห้องลอง
hông lorng

clothes/clothing
เสื้อผ้า
sêua pâa

shoes/footwear
รองเท้า
rorng táao

underwear
ชุดชั้นใน
chút chán nai

wallet
กระเป๋าเงิน
grà bpǎo nguhn

purse
กระเป๋าถือ
grà bpǎo těuu

umbrella
ร่ม
rôm

scent
กลิ่นหอม
glìn hǒrm

jewellery
เครื่องประดับ
krêuang bprà dàp

wool
ผ้าขนสัตว์
pâa kǒn sàt

denim
ผ้ายีนส์
pâa yeen

cotton
ฝ้าย
fâai

leather
หนัง
nǎng

silk
ผ้าไหม
pâa mǎi

size (clothing)
ไซส์
sái

size (shoe)
เบอร์
ber

to try on
ลอง
lorng

to fit
พอดี
por dee

CLOTHING

bikini
บิกินี่
bì gì nêe

blouse
เสื้อผู้หญิง
sêua pôo yǐng

coat
เสื้อนอก
sêua nôrk

dressing gown
เสื้อคลุม
sêua klum

dungarees
เอี๊ยม
íam

jacket
แจ็คเก็ต
jèk gèt

jeans
กางเกงยีนส์
gaang gayng yeen

jogging bottoms
กางเกงกีฬาขายาว
gaang gayng gee laa kǎa yaao

jumper
เสื้อแขนยาว
sêua kǎirn yaao

leggings
กางเกงเลกกิ้ง
gaang gayng lég gîng

pants
กางเกงใน
gaang gayng nai

pyjamas
ชุดนอน
chût norn

shirt
เสื้อเชิ้ต
sêua chért

shorts
กางเกงขาสั้น
gaang gayng kǎa sân

skirt
กระโปรง
grà bprohng

socks
ถุงเท้า
tǔng táao

sweatshirt
เสื้อยืดแขนยาว
sêua yêuut kǎirn yaao

swimsuit
ชุดว่ายน้ำ
chút wâai náam

(three-piece) suit
ชุดสูท
chút sòot

tie
เนคไท
nék tai

tights
ถุงน่อง
tǔng nông

trousers
กางเกงขายาว
gaang gayng kǎa yaao

T-shirt
เสื้อยืด
sêua yêuut

waterproof jacket
เสื้อกันฝน
sêua gan fǒn

ACCESSORIES

baseball cap
หมวกแก๊ป
mùak gáirp

belt
เข็มขัด
kěm kàt

bracelet
สร้อยข้อมือ
sôy kôr meuu

earrings
ต่างหู
dtàng hǒo

gloves
ถุงมือ
tǔng meuu

handbag
กระเป๋าถือ
grà bpǎo těuu

necklace
สร้อยคอ
sôy kor

scarf
ผ้าพันคอ
pâa pan kor

woolly hat
หมวกไหมพรม
mùak mǎi prom

FOOTWEAR

court shoes
รองเท้าหุ้มส้น
rorng táao hûm sôn

high heels
รองเท้าส้นสูง
rorng táao sôn sǒong

lace-up shoes
รองเท้าผูกเชือก
rorng táao pòok chêuak

sandals
รองเท้าสาน
rorng táao sǎan

slippers
รองเท้าแตะใส่ในบ้าน
rorng táao dtè sài nai bâan

trainers
รองเท้าผ้าใบ
rorng táao pâa bai

112

VOCABULARY

home improvements	painting	power tool
ปรับปรุงบ้าน	ทาสี	เครื่องมือไฟฟ้า
bpràp bprung bâan	taa sĕe	krêuang meuu fai fáa
joinery	decorating	to do DIY
วงกบไม้	แต่งบ้าน	ทำดีไอวาย
wong gòp máai	dtèng bâan	tam dee ai waai

HOME

hammer
ค้อน
kórn

light bulb
หลอดไฟ
lòrt fai

nails
ตะปู
dtà bpoo

nuts and bolts
น็อตเกลียวและหัวน็อต
nót gliaw lé hǔa nót

paint
สี
sĕe

paintbrush
แปรงทาสี
bprairng taa sĕe

pliers
คีม
keem

saw
เลื่อย
lêuay

screwdriver
ไขควง
kǎi kuang

screws
ตะปูเกลียว
dtà bpoo gliaw

spanner
ประแจ
bprà jair

stepladder
บันได
ban dai

tiles
กระเบื้อง
grà bêuang

wallpaper
วอลล์เปเปอร์
worn bpay bpêr

wrench
ประแจเลื่อน
bprà jair lêuan

GARDEN

garden fork
ส้อมพรวนใหญ่
sôrm pruan yài

gardening gloves
ถุงมือทำสวน
tǔng meuu tam sǔan

pruners
กรรไกรแต่งกิ่ง
gan grai dtèng gìng

spade
พลั่ว
plûa

trowel
ช้อนพรวน
chórn pruan

watering can
บัวรดน้ำ
bua rót náam

antique shop
ร้านขายของเก่า
ráan kǎai kǒrng gào

barber's
ร้านตัดผมชาย
ráan dtàt pǒm chaai

beauty salon
สถานเสริมความงาม
sà tǎan sěrm kwaam ngaam

bookshop
ร้านหนังสือ
ráan nang sěuu

car showroom
โชว์รูมรถ
choh room rót

coffee shop
ร้านกาแฟ
ráan gaa fair

convenience store
ร้านสะดวกซื้อ
ráan sà dùak séuu

department store
ห้างสรรพสินค้า
hâang sàp pá sǐn káa

electrical retailer
ร้านเครื่องไฟฟ้า
ráan krêuang fai fáa

estate agency
บริษัทนายหน้าบ้าน
และที่ดิน
bor rí sàt naai nâa bâan
lé têe din

florist's
ร้านดอกไม้
ráan dòrk máai

furniture store
ร้านเฟอร์นิเจอร์
ráan fer ní jêr

garden centre
ตลาดต้นไม้
dtà làat dtôn máai

gift shop
ร้านกิฟต์ช็อป
ráan gíp chóp

hairdresser's
ร้านทำผม
ráan tam pǒm

hardware shop
ร้านเครื่องมือช่าง
ráan krêuang meuu châng

jeweller's shop
ร้านเพชร
ráan pét

music shop
ร้านเครื่องดนตรี
ráan krêuang don dtree

optician's
ร้านตัดแว่น
ráan dtàt wên

pet shop
ร้านสัตว์เลี้ยง
ráan sàt líang

phone shop
ร้านมือถือ
ráan meuu tĕuu

shoe shop
ร้านรองเท้า
ráan rorng táao

stationer's
ร้านเครื่องเขียน
ráan krêuang kĭan

travel agent's
บริษัททัวร์
bor rí sàt tua

Business meetings, meals with friends, or courses of study...
whatever your day-to-day schedule looks like during your time in
Thailand, this section deals with the words and phrases you may
require when going on errands, planning outings, and going
about your everyday business.

coffee with milk
กาแฟใส่นม
gaa fair sài nom

handle
หู
hŏo

cup
ถ้วย
tûay

saucer
จานรอง
jaan rorng

YOU MIGHT SAY...

Where are you going?
คุณจะไปไหน
kun jà bpai năi

What time do you finish?
คุณเลิกกี่โมง
kun lêrk gèe mohng

What are you doing today/tonight?
วันนี้/คืนนี้ คุณทำอะไร
wan née/keuun née kun tam à rai

Are you free on Friday?
วันศุกร์นี้คุณว่างไหม
wan sùk née kun wâang mái

Where/When would you like to meet?
คุณอยากเจอกัน ที่ไหน/กี่โมง
kun yàak jer gan têe năi/gèe mohng

YOU MIGHT HEAR...

I'm at work/uni.
ผม/ฉัน อยู่ที่ ทำงาน/มหาวิทยาลัย
pŏm/chán yòo têe tam ngaan/má hăa wít tá yaa lai

I have a day off.
ผม/ฉัน มีวันหยุด
pŏm/chán mee wan yùt

I'm going to/planning to...
ผม/ฉัน จะไป.../วางแผนว่าจะ...
pŏm/chán jà bpai.../waang păirn wâa jà...

Let's meet at 6 p.m./at the restaurant.
เจอกัน 6 โมงเย็น/ที่ร้านอาหาร
jer gan hòk mohng yen/têe ráan aa hăan

I can't meet up at 11 a.m., sorry.
ตอน 11 โมงเช้า ผม/ฉัน ไปไม่ได้ ขอโทษ ครับ/ค่ะ
dtorn sìp èt mohng cháao pŏm/chán bpai mâi dâai kŏr tôht kráp/kâ

VOCABULARY

to wake up	to leave	to meet friends
ตื่นนอน	ออกจาก	ไปหาเพื่อน
dtèuun norn	òrk jàak	bpai hăa pêuan
to get dressed	to study	to go home
แต่งตัว	อ่านหนังสือเรียน	กลับบ้าน
dtèng dtua	àan nang sĕuu rian	glàp bâan
to arrive	to work	to go to bed
ไปถึง	ทำงาน	ไปนอน
bpai tĕung	tam ngaan	bpai norn

Many Thai people eat rice and side dishes for breakfast. Other popular breakfasts include Thai-style boiled rice soup (with added ingredients such as pork), Chinese-style rice porridge, and omelettes.

VOCABULARY

bread and butter	jam	to have breakfast
ขนมปังกับเนย	แยม	กินอาหารเช้า
kà nŏm bpang gàp noey	yairm	gin aa hăan cháao
bread and jam	to spread	to skip breakfast
ขนมปังกับแยม	ทา	ไม่กินอาหารเช้า
kà nŏm bpang gàp yairm	taa	mâi gin aa hăan cháao

chocolate spread
ช็อกโกแลต
chók goh lét

coffee
กาแฟ
gaa fair

coffee with milk
กาแฟใส่นม
gaa fair sài nom

congee
โจ๊ก
jóhk

deep fried breadstick
and soymilk
ปาท่องโก๋กับน้ำเต้าหู้
bpaa tôrng gŏh gàp nám
dtâo hôo

green tea
ชาเขียว
chaa kĭaw

muesli
มูสลี่
mút sà lêe

omelette
ไข่เจียว
kài jiaw

orange juice
น้ำส้ม
nám sôm

rice soup
ข้าวต้ม
kâao dtôm

steamed bun
ซาลาเปา
saa laa bpao

sticky rice and grilled pork
ข้าวเหนียวหมูปิ้ง
kâao nĭaw mŏo bpîng

tea
ชา
chaa

Unlike Western meals, Thai meals aren't divided into different courses. When eating in a group it is common to have multiple dishes on the table which are shared between diners. There is a huge variety of options for individuals and groups alike. Quick meals include noodle soup or rice with various toppings. Food courts and canteens offer a wide variety of freshly prepared dishes at affordable prices.

YOU MIGHT SAY...

What's for dinner?
เย็นนี้กินอะไร
yen née gin à rai

What time is lunch?
กินอาหารกลางวันกี่โมง
gin aa hǎan glaang wan gèe mohng

Can I try it?
ขอชิมได้ไหม
kǒr chim dâai mái

YOU MIGHT HEAR...

We're having ... for dinner.
เย็นนี้เราจะกิน...
yen née rao jà gin...

Lunch is at midday.
กินอาหารกลางวันตอนเที่ยง
gin aa hǎan glaang wan dtorn tîang

Dinner's ready!
ข้าวเย็นเสร็จแล้ว
kâao yen sèt láew

VOCABULARY

lunch
อาหารกลางวัน/
ข้าวเที่ยง
aa hǎan glaang wan/kâao tîang

dinner
อาหารเย็น/ข้าวเย็น
aa hǎan yen/kâao yen

supper
อาหารเย็น
aa hǎan yen

recipe
สูตร
sòot

to have lunch
กิน อาหารกลาง
วัน/ข้าวเที่ยง
gin aa hǎan glaang wan/kâao tîang

to have dinner
กินข้าวเย็น
gin kâao yen

YOU SHOULD KNOW...

Western-style food is widely available in big cities, shopping centres, and tourist areas.

STAPLE FOODS

bread
ขนมปัง
kà nŏm bpang

dumplings
ขนมจีบ
kà nŏm jèep

noodles
ก๋วยเตี๋ยว
gŭay dtĭaw

rice
ข้าว
kâao

rice and curry
ข้าวแกง
kâao gairng

rice noodles
เส้นก๋วยเตี๋ยว
sên gŭay dtĭaw

TYPICAL THAI DISHES

BBQ pork with rice
ข้าวหมูแดง
kâao mŏo dairng

chicken green curry
แกงเขียวหวานไก่
gairng kĭaw wăan gài

chicken/pork/beef panang curry
พะแนงไก่/หมู/เนื้อ
pá nairng gài/mŏo/néua

crispy catfish salad
ยำปลาดุกฟู
yam bplaa dùk foo

egg noodles with wontons and BBQ pork
บะหมี่เกี๊ยวหมูแดง
bà mèe gíaw mŏo dairng

fish curry with rice noodles
ขนมจีนน้ำยา
kà nŏm jeen nám yaa

122

fried mackerel with shrimp paste chilli sauce
น้ำพริกกะปิ ปลาทูทอด
nám prík gà bpì bplaa too tôrt

Hainanese chicken rice
ข้าวมันไก่
kâao man gài

hot and sour prawn soup
ต้มยำกุ้ง
dtôm yam gûng

minced pork omelette
ไข่เจียวหมูสับ
kài jiaw mǒo sàp

moo krata (barbecued pork)
หมูกระทะ
mǒo grà tá

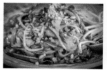

pad Thai
ผัดไทย
pàt tai

pork satay
หมูสะเต๊ะ
mǒo sà dté

prawns baked with vermicelli
กุ้งอบวุ้นเส้น
gûng òp wún sên

sour curry
แกงส้ม
gairng sôm

spicy glass noodle salad
ยำวุ้นเส้น
yam wún sên

spicy papaya salad
ส้มตำ
sôm dtam

stewed leg of pork with rice
ข้าวขาหมู
kâao kǎa mǒo

sticky rice with grilled chicken

ข้าวเหนียวไก่ย่าง

kâao nĭaw gài yâang

stir-fried broccoli with crispy pork belly

คะน้าหมูกรอบ

ká náa mŏo gròrp

stir-fried chicken/pork/ beef with holy basil

กะเพราไก่/หมู/เนื้อ

gà prao gài/mŏo/néua

stir-fried rice noodles in dark soy sauce

ผัดซีอิ๊ว

pàt see íw

stir-fried water spinach

ผักบุ้งไฟแดง

pàk bûng fai dairng

sweet chilli fried fish

ปลาราดพริก

bplaa râat prík

DESSERTS

banana in coconut milk

กล้วยบวชชี

glûay bùat chee

coconut pancake

ขนมครก

kà nŏm krók

egg yolk cooked in syrup

ทองหยิบ ทองหยอด ฝอยทอง

torng yìp torng yòrt fŏy torng

mango and sticky rice

ข้าวเหนียวมะม่วง

kâao nĭaw má mûang

mixed fresh fruit

ผลไม้รวม

pŏn la máai ruam

red ruby

ทับทิมกรอบ

táp tim gròrp

Thailand is renowned the world over for its cuisine, so it goes without saying that eating out is an important social experience in Thai culture.

YOU MIGHT SAY...

I'd like to make a reservation. อยากจองโต๊ะ ครับ/ค่ะ yàak jorng dtó kráp/kâ	I'd like... ผม/ฉัน อยากจะสั่ง... pŏm/chán yàak jà sàng...
A table for four, please. ขอโต๊ะสี่คน ครับ/ค่ะ kŏr dtó sèe kon kráp/kâ	I'm allergic to... ผม/ฉัน แพ้... pŏm/chán páir...
We're ready to order. สั่งอาหาร ครับ/ค่ะ sàng aa hăan kráp/kâ	I ordered a while ago and my food hasn't arrived. ผม/ฉัน สั่งอาหารนานแล้ว อาหารยังไม่มา pŏm/chán sàng aa hăan naan láew, aa hăan yang mâi maa
What would you recommend? มีอาหารอะไรแนะนำ mee aa hăan à rai né nam	
What are the specials today? วันนี้อาหารพิเศษอะไร wan née aa hăan pí sàyt à rai	This is not what I ordered. นี่ไม่ใช่อาหารที่เราสั่ง nêe mâi châi aa hăan têe rao sàng
	That was delicious. อาหารอร่อย aa hăan à ròy
Are there any vegetarian/vegan options? มี อาหารมังสวิรัติ/อาหารเจ ไหม mee aa hăan mang sà wì rát/aa hăan jay mái	May we have the bill, please? คิดเงินด้วย ครับ/ค่ะ kít nguhn dûay kráp/kâ

YOU SHOULD KNOW...

In smaller restaurants, free drinking water and ice may be available but it is often self-service.

At what time?
กี่โมง
gèe mohng

I would recommend...
ขอแนะนำ...
kŏr né nam...

How many people?
กี่คน ครับ/คะ
gèe kon kráp/ká

The specials today are...
อาหารพิเศษวันนี้มี...
aa hăan pí sàyt wan née mee...

Sorry, we're fully booked.
ขอโทษ ครับ/นะคะ โต๊ะเต็ม
หมดแล้ว
kŏr tôht kráp/ná ká dtó dtem mòt láew

I will let the chef know.
จะบอกในครัวให้ ครับ/ค่ะ
jà bòrk nai krua hâi kráp/kâ

Would you like anything to drink?
รับน้ำอะไร ครับ/คะ
ráp náam à rai kráp/ká

Enjoy your meal!
ทานให้อร่อย ครับ/ค่ะ
taan hâi à ròy kráp/kâ

Are you ready to order?
สั่งเลยไหม ครับ/คะ
sàng loey mái kráp/ká

VOCABULARY

set menu	vegetarian	to order
อาหารชุด	มังสวิรัติ	สั่ง
aa hăan chút	mang sà wì rát	sàng
daily specials	vegan	to ask for the bill
อาหารพิเศษประจำ	เจ	คิดเงิน
วัน	jay	kít nguhn
aa hăan pí sàyt bprà jam		
wan		
	gluten-free	to be served
	ไม่ใส่กลูเตน	เสิร์ฟให้
service charge	mâi sài gloo dtayn	sèrp hâi
เซอร์วิสชาร์จ		
ser wít cháat		

TABLE SETTING

straw
หลอด
lòrt

spoon and fork
ช้อนส้อม
chórn sôrm

serving bowl
ชาม
chaam

water glass
แก้วน้ำ
gâew náam

plate
จาน
jaan

bowl
ถ้วย
tûay

GENERAL

bar
บาร์
baa

bill
บิล
bin

ice
น้ำแข็ง
nám kĕng

menu
เมนู
may noo

noodle condiments
พวงพริก
puang prík

pepper pot
ขวดพริกไทย
kùat prík tai

tablecloth
ผ้าปูโต๊ะ
pâa bpoo dtó

toothpicks
ไม้จิ้มฟัน
máai jîm fan

waiter/waitress
พนักงานเสิร์ฟ
pá nák ngaan sèrp

FAST FOOD | อาหารจานด่วน

Western-style fast food is available in big cities and tourist areas, and there are also many local specialities sold by street and market vendors you can enjoy on the go.

YOU MIGHT SAY...

I'd like to order, please.
สั่งอาหารหน่อย ครับ/ค่ะ
sàng aa hăan nòy kráp/kâ

Do you deliver?
ส่งอาหารไหม
sòng aa hăan măi

I'm sitting in/taking away.
ทานที่นี่/เอากลับบ้าน
taan têe nêe/ao glàp bâan

That's everything, thanks.
อาหารครบแล้ว ขอบคุณ ครับ/ค่ะ
aa hăan króp láew kòrp kun kráp/kâ

YOU MIGHT HEAR...

Can I help you?
รับอะไร ครับ/คะ
ráp à rai kráp/ká

Sit-in or takeaway?
ทานที่นี่หรือกลับบ้าน
taan têe nêe rěuu glàp bâan

We do/don't do delivery.
ร้านเราส่งอาหาร/ไม่ส่งอาหาร
ráan rao sòng aa hăan/mâi sòng aa hăan

Would you like anything else?
รับอะไรเพิ่มไหม ครับ/คะ
ráp à rai pêrm măi kráp/ká

VOCABULARY

fast-food chain
ร้านอาหาร
แฟรนไชส์
ráan aa hăan frairn chái

food stall
แผงขายอาหาร
păirng kăai aa hăan

street food
อาหารริมทาง
aa hăan rim taang

vendor
คนขาย
kon kăai

drive-thru
ขับรถเข้าไปสั่ง
อาหาร
kàp rót kâo bpai sàng aa
hăan

an order to go/
a takeaway
อาหารสั่งกลับบ้าน
aa hăan sàng glàp bâan

delivery charge
ค่าส่ง
kâa sòng

to place an order
สั่งอาหาร
sàng aa hăan

to collect an order
มารับอาหาร
maa ráp aa hăan

barbecued pork/
chicken/beef
บาร์บีคิว หมู/ไก่/เนื้อ
baa bee kiw mŏo/gài/
néua

burger
เบอร์เกอร์
ber ger

fried chicken
ไก่ทอด
gài tôrt

fries
มันฝรั่งทอด
man fà ràng tôrt

grilled chicken
ไก่ย่าง
gài yâang

grilled pork skewer
หมูปิ้ง
mŏo bpîng

pizza
พิซซ่า
pít sâa

salad
สลัด
sà làt

sandwich
แซนวิช
sairn wít

set meal box
อาหารกล่อง
aa hăan glòrng

sushi
ซูชิ
soo chí

wonton soup
เกี๊ยวน้ำ
gíaw náam

COMMUNICATION AND IT | การสื่อสารและไอที

Technology plays a huge role in people's everyday lives. A mere click, tap, or swipe helps us to stay in touch with friends and family, keep up to date with what's going on, and find the information we need.

YOU MIGHT SAY/HEAR...

I'll give you a call later.
แล้ว ผม/ฉัน จะโทรหานะ
láew pǒm/chán jà toh hǎa ná

I'll email you.
ผม/ฉัน จะอีเมลหาคุณ
pǒm/chán jà ee mayw hǎa kun

What's your number?
เบอร์โทรของคุณอะไร
ber toh kǒrng kun à rai

This is a bad line.
สัญญาณไม่ดี
sǎn yaan mâi dee

I don't have any signal.
ผม/ฉัน ไม่มีสัญญาณ
pǒm/chán mâi mee sǎn yaan

May I have your email address?
ผม/ฉัน ขออีเมลคุณได้ไหม
pǒm/chán kǒr ee mayw kǒrng kun dâai mái

The website address is...
เว็บไซต์...
wép sái...

What's the WiFi password?
พาสเวิร์ดไวไฟอะไร
páat wért wai fai à rai

It's all one word.
ติดกันทั้งหมด
dtìt gan táng mòt

It's upper/lower case.
ตัวใหญ่/ตัวเล็ก
dtua yài/dtua lék

VOCABULARY

post ไปรษณีย์ bprai sà nee	email อีเมล ee mayw	internet อินเทอร์เน็ต in ter nèt
social media โซเชียลมีเดีย soh chiaw mee dia	email address ที่อยู่อีเมล têe yòo ee mayw	WiFi ไวไฟ wai fai

website
เว็บไซต์
wép sái

landline
โทรศัพท์บ้าน
toh rá sàp bâan

cable
เคเบิล
kay bern

link
ลิงก์
líng

phone call
โทรศัพท์
toh rá sàp

to make a phone call
ไปโทรศัพท์
bpai toh rá sàp

icon
ไอคอน
ai korn

text message
ข้อความ
kôr kwaam

to send a text
ส่งข้อความ
sòng kôr kwaam

mouse
เมาส์
máo

voice mail
ข้อความเสียง
kôr kwaam sĭang

to post (online)
โพสต์
póht

keyboard
คีย์บอร์ด
kee bòrt

touchscreen
ทัชสกรีน
tát sà green

to download/upload
ดาวน์โหลด/
อัปโหลด
daao lòht/àp lòht

app
แอป
èp

screen
หน้าจอ
nâa jor

to charge your phone
ชาร์จมือถือ
cháat meuu tĕuu

data
ดาต้า
daa dtâa

button
ปุ่ม
bpùm

to switch on/off
เปิด/ปิด
bpèrt/bpìt

mobile phone
โทรศัพท์มือถือ
toh rá sàp meuu tĕuu

battery
แบตเตอรี่
bèt dter rêe

to click on
คลิก
klík

YOU SHOULD KNOW...

Internet cafés were once very common but the boom in portable devices has reduced the need for these. If you wish to buy a smartphone in Thailand that you plan to use in the UK afterwards, try to make sure it supports the frequency bands for mobile internet used by your UK network.

charger
ที่ชาร์จ
têe cháat

computer
คอมพิวเตอร์
korm piw dtêr

mouse mat
แผ่นรองเมาส์
pèn rorng máo

phone case
เคสมือถือ
káyt meuu těuu

power pack
เพาเวอร์แบงค์
pao wêr báirng

SIM card
ซิมการ์ด
sim gàat

smartphone
สมาร์ทโฟน
sà màat fohn

tablet
แท็ปเล็ต
tèp lét

wireless router
เราเตอร์ไร้สาย
rao dter rái sǎai

Thai children usually attend nursery school, followed by 6 years of primary education. Secondary school is divided into two levels, each lasting 3 years. If a student chooses not to attend senior secondary school, there are other vocational options.

YOU MIGHT SAY...

What are you studying?
คุณเรียนอะไร
kun rian à rai

What year are you in?
คุณเรียนปีอะไร
kun rian bpee à rai

What's your favourite subject?
คุณชอบเรียนวิชาอะไรมากที่สุด
kun chôrp rian wí chaa à rai mâak têe sùt

YOU MIGHT HEAR...

I'm studying...
ผม/ฉัน เรียน...
pŏm/chán rian...

I'm in Year 6/my final year.
ผม/ฉัน เรียน ม. 6/ปีสุดท้าย
pŏm/chán rian mor hòk/bpee sùt táai

I have an assignment.
ผม/ฉัน มีงานที่ต้องทำ
pŏm/chán mee ngaan têe dtông tam

VOCABULARY

nursery school
โรงเรียนอนุบาล
rohng rian à nú baan

primary school
โรงเรียนประถม
rohng rian bprà tŏm

junior/senior
secondary school
โรงเรียนมัธยม ต้น/
ปลาย
rohng rian mát tá yom
dtôn/bplaai

college
วิทยาลัย
wít tá yaa lai

university
มหาวิทยาลัย
má hăa wít tá yaa lai

headteacher
ครูใหญ่
kroo yài

janitor
ภารโรง
paan rohng

timetable
ตารางเรียน
dtaa raang rian

lesson
บทเรียน
bòt rian

lecture
อาจารย์
aa jaan

tutorial
เรียนติว
rian dtiw

assignment
งานที่ต้องทำ
ngaan têe dtông tam

homework
การบ้าน
gaan bâan

exam
สอบ
sòrp

degree
ปริญญา
bpà rin yaa

undergraduate
ปริญญาตรี
bpà rin yaa dtree

postgraduate
บัณฑิตศึกษา
ban dìt sèuk săa

assembly hall
หอประชุม
hŏr bprà chum

playing field
สนามกีฬา
sà năam gee laa

playground
สนามเด็กเล่น
sà năam dèk lên

halls of residence
หอพักของมหาวิทยาลัย
hŏr pák kŏrng má hăa
wít tá yaa lai

student union
สโมสรนักศึกษา
sà moh sŏrn nák sèuk săa

student card
บัตรนักศึกษา
bàt nák sèuk săa

school/university
uniform
เครื่องแบบ
นักเรียน/นักศึกษา
krêuang bàirp nák rian/
nák sèuk săa

to learn
เรียน
rian

to teach
สอน
sŏrn

to revise
ทบทวน
tóp tuan

to sit an exam
เข้าสอบ
kâo sòrp

to graduate
เรียนจบ
rian jòp

to study
เรียน
rian

SCHOOL

classroom
ห้องเรียน
hông rian

colouring pencils
ดินสอสี
din sŏr sĕe

eraser
ยางลบ
yaang lóp

exercise book
สมุดแบบฝึกหัด
sà mùt bàirp fèuk hàt

felt-tip pens
สีเมจิก
sěe may jìk

fountain pen
ปากกาหมึกซึม
bpàak gaa mèuk seum

hole punch
ที่เจาะกระดาษ
têe jò grà dàat

paper
กระดาษ
grà dàat

paper clip
คลิป
klíp

pen
ปากกา
bpàak gaa

pencil
ดินสอ
din sǒr

pencil case
กระเป๋าดินสอ
grà bpǎo din sǒr

pupil
นักเรียน
nák rian

ruler
ไม้บรรทัด
máai ban tát

schoolbag
กระเป๋านักเรียน
grà bpǎo nák rian

scissors
กรรไกร
gan grai

sharpener
กบเหลาดินสอ
gòp lǎo din sǒr

stapler
ที่เย็บกระดาษ
têe yép grà dàat

teacher
ครู
kroo

textbook
หนังสือเรียน
nang sěuu rian

whiteboard
ไวท์บอร์ด
wai bòrt

HIGHER EDUCATION

campus
แคมปัส
kairm bpàt

canteen
โรงอาหาร
rohng aa hǎan

lecture hall
ห้องบรรยาย
hông ban yaai

lecturer
อาจารย์
aa jaan

library
ห้องสมุด
hông sà mùt

student
นักศึกษา
nák sèuk sǎa

Usual office hours are 8 a.m. to 5 p.m. with a one-hour lunch break. There are a number of public holidays throughout the year when most office workers can take the day off.

YOU MIGHT SAY/HEAR...

Can we arrange a meeting?
เรานัดประชุมกันได้ไหม
rao nát bprà chum gan dâai mái

May I speak to...?
ขอสายคุณ ... ครับ/ค่ะ
kŏr săai kun ... kráp/kâ

Can you send me...?
คุณช่วยส่ง ... ให้ได้ไหม
kun chûay sòng ... hâi dâai mái

I have a meeting with...
ผม/ฉัน มีประชุมกับ...
pŏm/chán mee bprà chum gàp...

Mr/Ms ... is on the phone.
คุณ ... โทรศัพท์อยู่
kun ... toh rá sàp yòo

Here's my business card.
นี่นามบัตรของ ผม/ดิฉัน
nêe naam bàt kŏrng pŏm/dì chán

Who's calling?
ใครโทรมา
krai toh maa

Can I call you back?
ขอโทรกลับได้ไหม ครับ/คะ
kŏr toh glàp dâai mái kráp/ká

VOCABULARY

manager
ผู้จัดการ
pôo jàt gaan

staff
พนักงาน
pá nák ngaan

colleague
เพื่อนร่วมงาน
pêuan rûam ngaan

client
ลูกค้า
lôok káa

human resources
ทรัพยากรบุคคล
sáp pá yaa gorn bùk kon

spreadsheet
โปรแกรมสเปรดชีต
bproh grairm sà bprèt chéet

presentation
การนำเสนอ
gaan nam sà něr

report
รายงาน
raai ngaan

meeting
ประชุม
bprà chum

conference call
ประชุมทางโทรศัพท์
bprà chum taang toh rá sàp

attachment
เอกสารแนบท้าย
àyk gà sǎan nâirp táai

to give a presentation
นำเสนอ
nam sà něr

video conference
ประชุมทางวิดีโอ
bprà chum taang wí dee oh

username
ชื่อผู้ใช้
chêuu pôo chái

to hold a meeting
จัดประชุม
jàt bprà chum

inbox
อินบ็อกซ์
in bòk

password
พาสเวิร์ด
páat wért

to log on/off
ล็อกอิน/ล็อกออฟ
lók in/lók óop

YOU SHOULD KNOW...

The hierarchical elements of Thai language and culture are important in the office environment. Thus it is important to use polite language and perform the wai (a slight bow with the palms pressed together) when talking to senior staff.

desk
โต๊ะทำงาน
dtó tam ngaan

filing cabinet
ตู้เก็บเอกสาร
dtôo gèp àyk gà sǎan

folder
แฟ้ม
fáirm

in/out tray
ถาด รับ/ส่ง เอกสาร
tàat ráp/sòng àyk gà sǎan

laptop
แล็ปท็อปคอมพิวเตอร์
lép tóp korm piw dtêr

notepad
กระดาษจด
grà dàat jòt

photocopier
เครื่องถ่ายเอกสาร
krêuang tàai àyk gà săn

printer
ปริ้นเตอร์
bprín dtêr

ring binder
แฟ้มห่วง
fáirm hùang

scanner
เครื่องสแกนเนอร์
krêuang sà gairn nêr

sticky notes
โพสต์อิท
póht ít

sticky tape
เทปกาว
táyp gaao

telephone
โทรศัพท์
toh rá sàp

swivel chair
เก้าอี้สำนักงาน
gâo êe săm nák ngaan

USB stick
แฟลชไดรฟ์
flét drái

Banks are normally open during the day from Monday to Friday, though opening hours may vary. In big cities and tourist areas there are also small kiosks offering various banking services. You may find that currency exchange stores offer more competitive rates than the banks.

YOU MIGHT SAY...

I'd like to...
ผม/ดิฉัน อยากจะ...
pŏm/dì chán yàak jà...

... register for online banking.
... ลงทะเบียนออนไลน์แบงค์กิ้ง
... long tá bian orn lai bairng gîng

Is there a fee for this service?
มีค่าบริการไหม
mee kâa bor rí gaan mái

I need to cancel my debit/credit card.
ผม/ฉัน อยากยกเลิกบัตร เดบิต/เครดิต ครับ/ค่ะ
pŏm/chán yàak yók lêrk bàt day bìt/ kray dìt kráp/kâ

YOU MIGHT HEAR...

May I see your ID, please?
ขอดู บัตรประจำตัว/พาสปอร์ต ครับ/ค่ะ
kŏr doo bàt bprà jam dtua/páat sà bpòrt kráp/kâ

How much would you like to withdraw/deposit?
ถอน/ฝาก เงินเท่าไหร่ ครับ/ค่ะ
tŏrn/fàak nguhn tâo rài kráp/ká

Could you enter your PIN, please?
กดรหัสได้เลย ครับ/ค่ะ
gòt rá hàt dâai loey kráp/kâ

You must fill out an application form.
คุณต้องกรอกใบสมัคร
kun dtông gròrk bai sà màk

VOCABULARY

branch
สาขา
săa kăa

cashier
แคชเชียร์
két chia

online banking
ออนไลน์แบงค์กิ้ง
orn lai bairng gîng

bank account
บัญชีธนาคาร
ban chee tá naa kaan

current account
บัญชีกระแสรายวัน
ban chee grà săir raai wan

savings account
บัญชีออมทรัพย์
ban chee orm sáp

account number
หมายเลขบัญชี
măai lâyk ban chee

bank balance
ยอดเงินฝาก
yôrt nguhn fàak

bank statement
สเตทเมนต์บัญชี
sà dtàyt mén ban chee

overdraft
โอเวอร์ดราฟต์
oh wêr dráap

loan
เงินกู้
nguhn gôo

to withdraw funds
ถอนเงิน
tŏrn nguhn

bank transfer
โอนเงิน
ohn nguhn

mortgage
จำนอง
jam norng

to make a deposit
ฝากเงิน
fàak nguhn

chequebook
สมุดเช็ค
sà mùt chék

interest
ดอกเบี้ย
dòrk bîa

to open an account
เปิดบัญชี
bpèrt ban chee

currency
เงินตรา
nguhn dtraa

to borrow
ขอยืม
kŏr yeuum

to change money
แลกเงิน
lâirk nguhn

ATM
เอทีเอ็ม
ay tee em

banknotes
เงินแบงค์/ธนบัตร
nguhn béng/tá ná bàt

bureau de change
บริการแลกเงิน
bor rí gaan lâirk nguhn

debit/credit card
บัตร เดบิต/เครดิต
bàt day bìt/kray dìt

exchange rate
อัตราแลกเปลี่ยน
àt dtraa lâirk bplìan

safety deposit box
ตู้เซฟ
dtôo sáyp

THE POST OFFICE | ที่ทำการไปรษณีย์

Post offices offer a wide range of global shipping options. Sometimes post office kiosks can be found in shopping centres.

YOU MIGHT SAY...

I'd like to send this by airmail.
ส่งทางแอร์เมล ครับ/ค่ะ
sòng taang air mayw kráp/kâ

Can I get a receipt, please?
ขอใบเสร็จรับเงิน ครับ/ค่ะ
kŏr bai sèt ráp nguhn kráp/kâ

How long will delivery take?
ใช้เวลากี่วัน
chái way laa gèe wan

I'd like 4 stamps, please.
ขอแสตมป์ 4 ดวง ครับ/ค่ะ
kŏr sà dtáirm sèe duang kráp/kâ

YOU MIGHT HEAR...

Place it on the scales, please.
วางบนตราชั่ง ครับ/ค่ะ
waang bon dtraa châng kráp/kâ

What are the contents?
ข้างในมีอะไร
kâang nai mee à rai

What is the value of this parcel?
มูลค่าของที่ส่งเท่าไหร่
moon lá kâa kŏrng têe sòng tâo rài

Here is your receipt.
ใบเสร็จรับเงิน ครับ/ค่ะ
bai sèt ráp nguhn kráp/kâ

VOCABULARY

address
ที่อยู่
têe yòo

postal van
รถขนส่งไปรษณีย์
rót kŏn sòng bprai sà nee

mail
ไปรษณีย์
bprai sà nee

airmail
แอร์เมล.
air mayw

courier
บริการรับส่ง
ไปรษณีย์
bor rí gaan ráp sòng
bprai sà nee

to post
ส่ง
sòng

to send
ส่ง
sòng

to return a package
ส่งของคืน
sòng kŏrng keuun

YOU SHOULD KNOW...

The Thai postal service is generally efficient and reliable. Other international courier services are also available.

box
กล่อง
glòrng

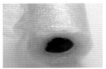

bubble wrap
แผ่นกันกระแทก
pèn gan grà tâirk

envelope
ซอง
sorng

letter
จดหมาย
jòt măai

package
ห่อพัสดุ
hòr pát sà dù

postal worker
พนักงานไปรษณีย์
pá nák ngaan bprai sà nee

postbox
ตู้ไปรษณีย์
dtôo bprai sà nee

postcard
โปสการ์ด
bpòht gàat

stamp
แสตมป์
sà dtáirm

YOU MIGHT SAY...

How do I get to the centre of town?
ไปในเมืองยังไง ครับ/คะ
bpai nai meuang yang gai kráp/ká

I need to go to...
ผม/ฉัน ต้องไป...
pŏm/chán dtông bpai...

I'd like to visit...
ผม/ฉัน อยากไปเที่ยว...
pŏm/chán yàak bpai tîaw...

What are the opening hours?
เปิดกี่โมงถึงกี่โมง
bpèrt gèe mohng tĕung gèe mohng

YOU MIGHT HEAR...

It's open between ... and...
เปิดตั้งแต่ ... ถึง...
bpèrt dtâng dtàir ... tĕung...

It's closed on Mondays.
ปิดวันจันทร์
bpìt wan jan

PLACES OF IMPORTANCE

café
ร้านกาแฟ
ráan gaa fair

church
โบสถ์คริสต์
bòht krít

cinema
โรงหนัง/โรงภาพยนตร์
rohng năng/rohng pâap pá yon

conference centre
ศูนย์การประชุม
sŏon gaan bprà chum

courthouse
ศาล
săan

dry cleaner's
ร้านซักแห้ง
ráan sák hâirng

fire station
สถานีดับเพลิง
sà tăa nee dàp plerng

fountain
น้ำพุ
náam pú

hospital
โรงพยาบาล
rohng pá yaa baan

hotel
โรงแรม
rohng rairm

library
ห้องสมุด
hông sà mùt

mosque
มัสยิด
mát sà yìt

office block
อาคารสำนักงาน
aa kaan săm nák ngaan

park
สวนสาธารณะ
sŭan săa taa rá ná

playground
สนามเด็กเล่น
sà năam dèk lên

police station
สถานีตำรวจ
sà tăa nee dtam rùat

retail park
ย่านการค้า
yâan gaan káa

town hall
ศาลากลาง
săa laa glaang

A day trip, a break away, a night out, maybe even a night in – we all like to spend our free time differently. It's also a common topic of conversation with friends and colleagues; who doesn't like talking about holidays, hobbies, and how they like to hang out?

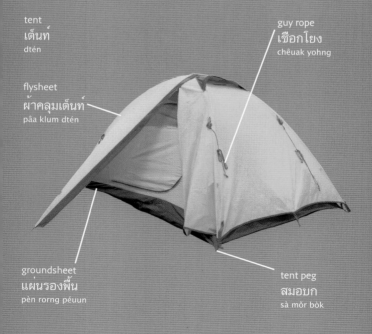

tent
เต็นท์
dtén

guy rope
เชือกโยง
chêuak yohng

flysheet
ผ้าคลุมเต็นท์
pâa klum dtén

groundsheet
แผ่นรองพื้น
pèn rorng péuun

tent peg
สมอบก
sà mŏr bòk

YOU MIGHT SAY...

What would you like to do?
คุณชอบทำอะไร
kun chôrp tam à rai

What do you do in your spare time?
เวลาว่างคุณชอบทำอะไร
way laa wâang kun chôrp tam à rai

Have you got any hobbies?
คุณมีงานอดิเรกไหม
kun mee ngaan à dì ràyk mái

Are you sporty/creative/musical?
คุณเป็นคนชอบเล่นกีฬา/ศิลปะ/ดนตรีไหม
kun bpen kon chôrp lên gee laa/sĭn lá bpà/don dtree mái

Do you enjoy...?
คุณชอบ ... ไหม
kun chôrp ... mái

YOU MIGHT HEAR...

My hobbies include...
งานอดิเรกของ ผม/ฉัน คือ...
ngaan à dì ràyk kŏrng pŏm/chán keuu...

I like...
ผม/ฉัน ชอบ...
pŏm/chán chôrp...

I really enjoy...
ผม/ฉัน ชอบ ... มาก
pŏm/chán chôrp ... mâak

It's not for me.
ผม/ฉัน ไม่ชอบเลย
pŏm/chán mâi chôrp loey

I have/don't have a lot of spare time.
ผม/ฉัน มี/ไม่มี เวลาว่างมาก
pŏm/chán mee/mâi mee way laa wâang mâak

VOCABULARY

activity
กิจกรรม
gìt jà gam

hobby/pastime
งานอดิเรก
ngaan à dì ràyk

to be interested in
สนใจ
sŏn jai

to pass the time
ทำเวลาว่าง
tam way laa wâang

to relax
พักผ่อน
pák pòrn

to enjoy
ชอบ
chôrp

cooking
ทำอาหาร
tam aahăan

DIY
ทำงานช่าง
tam ngaan châng

gaming
เล่นเกม
lên gaym

jogging
วิ่ง
wîng

listening to music
ฟังเพลง
fang playng

photography
การถ่ายภาพ
gaan tàai pâap

reading
อ่านหนังสือ
àan nangsĕuu

shopping
ซื้อของ
séuu kŏrng

sports
เล่นกีฬา
lên gee laa

travelling
เดินทางท่องเที่ยว
dern taang tông tîaw

walking
เดินป่า
dern bpàa

watching TV/films
ดูทีวี/หนัง
doo tee wee/năng

Thailand is one of the most popular tourist destinations in the world – given its fascinating culture and the wealth of sightseeing opportunities for visitors, it's easy to see why.

YOU MIGHT SAY...

How much is it to get in?
ค่าเข้าเท่าไหร่
kâa kâo tâo rài

Is there a discount for...?
มีส่วนลดให้ ... ไหม
mee sùan lót hâi ... mái

Are there sightseeing tours?
มีบริษัทนำเที่ยวไหม
mee bor rí sàt nam tîaw mái

YOU MIGHT HEAR...

Entry costs ... baht.
ค่าเข้า ... บาท
kâa kâo ... bàat

There is a guided tour you can book.
นี่คือทัวร์มีไกด์ที่คุณจองได้
nêe keuu tua mee gái têe kun jorng dâai

Audio guides are/are not available.
มี/ไม่มีเสียงบรรยายนำทาง
mee/mâi mee sĭang ban yaai nam taang

VOCABULARY

tourist
นักท่องเที่ยว
nák tông tîaw

tourist attraction
สถานที่ท่องเที่ยว
sà tăan têe tông tîaw

tourist office
ศูนย์บริการ
นักท่องเที่ยว
sŏon bor rí gaan nák
tông tîaw

excursion
การไปเที่ยว
gaan bpai tîaw

historic site
สถานที่สำคัญทาง
ประวัติศาสตร์
sà tăan têe săm kan
taang bprà wàt dtì sàat

to visit
ไปเที่ยว
bpai tîaw

YOU SHOULD KNOW...

Some religious sites require visitors to dress modestly and you may be asked to remove your shoes before entering. Long skirts and trousers are advised but sarongs may be available at some attractions for visitors to use if required.

art gallery
ที่แสดงศิลปะ
têe sà dairng sĭn lá bpà

audio guide
เสียงบรรยายนำทาง
sĭang ban yaai nam taang

camera
กล้องถ่ายรูป
glông tàai rôop

city map
แผนที่เมือง
păirn têe meuang

gardens
สวน
sŭan

guidebook
หนังสือนำเที่ยว
nang sĕuu nam tîaw

monument
อนุสาวรีย์
à nú săa wá ree

museum
พิพิธภัณฑ์
pí pít ta pan

palace
วัง
wang

sightseeing bus
รถบัสชมเมือง
rót bát chom meuang

temple
วัด
wát

tour guide
ไกด์นำเที่ยว
gái nam tîaw

When it comes to nightlife in Thailand's towns and cities, check the local tourist office for information on local events and venues.

YOU MIGHT SAY...

What is there to do at night?
กลางคืนมีอะไรให้ทำบ้าง
glaang keuun mee à rai hâi tam bâang

What's on at the cinema/theatre?
มีอะไรให้ดูที่โรงหนัง/โรงละคร
mee à rai hâi doo thêe rohng năng/
rohng lá korn

Where are the best bars/clubs?
บาร์/คลับที่ดีที่สุดอยู่ที่ไหน
baa/klàp têe dee têe sùt yòo têe năi

Do you want to go for a drink?
คุณอยากไปดื่มด้วยกันไหม
kun yàak bpai dèuum dûay gan mái

Do you want to go and see a...?
คุณอยากไปดู ... ไหม
kun yàak bpai doo ... mái

Are there tickets for...?
มีตั๋วของ ... ไหม
mee dtŭa kŏrng ... mái

Two seats in the stalls, please.
ขอตั๋วสองใบ
kŏr dtŭa sŏrng bai

What time does it start?
เริ่มกี่โมง
rêrm gèe mohng

YOU MIGHT HEAR...

I'm going for a few drinks/to the theatre/dancing.
ผม/ฉัน จะไปดื่มนิดหน่อย/ไปดู
ละครเวที/ไปเต้นรำ
pŏm/chán jà bpai dèuum nít nòy/bpai
doo lá korn way tee/bpai tên ram

There's a film/show I'd like to see.
มีหนัง/การแสดงที่ ผม/ฉัน
อยากดู
mee năng/gaan sà dairng têe pŏm/
chán yàak doo

There are no tickets left.
ไม่มีตั๋วแล้ว
mâi mee dtŭa láew

It begins at 7 o'clock.
เริ่มตอนเจ็ดโมง
rêrm dtorn jèt mohng

Please turn off your mobile phones.
กรุณาปิดโทรศัพท์มือถือ
gà rú naa bpìt toh rá sàp meuu tĕuu

VOCABULARY

a drink
เครื่องดื่ม
krêuang dèuum

nightlife
เที่ยวกลางคืน
tîaw glaang keuun

party
งานเลี้ยง
ngaan líang

show
การแสดง
gaan sà dairng

film
หนัง/ภาพยนตร์
năng/pâap pá yon

play
ละคร
lá korn

festival
เทศกาล
tâyt sà gaan

box office
ที่ขายตั๋ว/บัตร
têe kăai tŭa/bàt

to socialize
เข้าสังคม
kâo săng kom

to go out
ไปเที่ยว
bpai tîaw

to order food/drinks
สั่งอาหาร/เครื่องดื่ม
sàng aa hăan/krêuang
dèuum

to see a show
ดูการแสดง
doo gaan sà dairng

to watch a film
ดูหนัง
doo năng

to go dancing
ไปเต้นรำ
bpai tên ram

to enjoy oneself
ไปสนุกกัน
bpai sà nùk gan

YOU SHOULD KNOW...

In Thailand it is common to enjoy a meal and drinks with friends in open-air restaurants. Sometimes there is also a live band. Don't be surprised if the waiting staff put ice in your beer – in Thailand this is common due to the hot weather.

ballet
บัลเล่ต์
ban lây

bar
บาร์
baa

cabaret show
โชว์คาบาเร่
choh kaa baa rây

cinema
โรงหนัง
rohng năng

coffee house
ร้านกาแฟ
ráan gaa fair

concert
คอนเสิร์ต
korn sèrt

karaoke
คาราโอเกะ
kaa raa oh gè

live music
ดนตรีสด
don dtree sòt

musical
ละครเพลง
lá korn playng

nightclub
ไนท์คลับ
nái kláp

night market
ตลาดกลางคืน
dtà làat glaang keuun

opera
โอเปร่า
oh bpay râa

restaurant
ร้านอาหาร
ráan aa hăan

temple fair
งานวัด
ngaan wát

theatre
โรงละคร
rohng lá korn

With Thailand being such a popular tourist destination there is a wide range of accommodation options to choose from. These include high-end hotels and smaller guest houses popular with backpackers. Another option for the more adventurous traveller is to book a homestay with locals.

YOU MIGHT SAY...

I have a reservation.
ผม/ฉัน จองมาแล้ว
pŏm/chán jorng maa láew

Have you got rooms available?
คุณมีห้องว่างไหม
kun mee hông wâang mái

How much is it per night?
ค่าห้องคืนละเท่าไหร่
kâa hông keuun lá tâo rài

Is breakfast included?
รวมอาหารเช้าไหม
ruam aa hăan cháao mái

I'd like to check in/out, please.
ผม/ฉัน อยากจะเช็กอิน/เอาท์
pŏm/chán yàak jà chék in/áo

I'd like to book a single/double room, please.
ผม/ฉัน ต้องการจองห้องเดี่ยว/ห้องคู่
pŏm/chán dtông gaan jorng hông dìaw/hông kôo

What time is breakfast served?
อาหารเช้าเริ่มกี่โมง
aa hăan cháao rêrm gèe mohng

What time do I have to check out?
ผม/ฉัน ต้องเช็กเอาท์เวลากี่โมง
pŏm/chán tông chék áo way laa gèe mohng

Could I upgrade my room?
ผม/ฉัน ขออัปเกรดห้องได้ไหม
pŏm/chán kŏr àp gràyt hông dâai mái

I need fresh towels for my room.
ผม/ฉัน ขอผ้าเช็ดตัวใหม่ในห้องด้วย
pŏm/chán kŏr pâa chét dtua mài nai hông dûay

I've lost my key.
ผม/ฉัน ทำกุญแจหาย
pŏm/chán tam gun jair hăai

I'd like to make a complaint.
ผม/ฉัน มีข้อร้องเรียน
pŏm/chán mee kôr rórng rian

YOU SHOULD KNOW...

When checking in to your hotel, you will be required to show your passport and in some cases you may have to pay a security deposit.

YOU MIGHT HEAR...

We have/don't have rooms available.
มี/ไม่มีห้องว่าง
mee/mâi mee hông wâang

May I have your room number, please?
ขอเบอร์ห้องด้วยครับ/ค่ะ
kŏr ber hông dûay kráp/kâ

Our rates are ... baht.
ค่าห้อง ... บาท
kâa hông ... bàat

May I see your documents, please?
ขอดูเอกสารเดินทางหน่อย
ครับ/ค่ะ
kŏr doo àyk gà săan dern taang nòy
kráp/kâ

Breakfast is/is not included.
รวม/ไม่รวมอาหารเช้า
ruam/mâi ruam aa hăan cháao

You may check in after...
คุณเช็กอินได้หลัง ... โมง
kun chék in dâai lăng ... mohng

Breakfast is served at...
อาหารเช้าเริ่มเวลา ... โมง
aa hăan cháao rêrm way laa ... mohng

You must check out before...
คุณต้องเช็กเอาท์ก่อน ... โมง
kun dtông chék áo gòrn ... mohng

VOCABULARY

guest house
เกสท์เฮาส์
gàyt hao

half board
พร้อมอาหารเช้า
และอาหารเย็น
prórm aa hăan cháao lé
aa hăan yen

per person per night
ต่อคนต่อคืน
tòr kon tòr keuun

bed and breakfast
ที่พักพร้อมอาหาร
เช้า
têe pák prórm aa hăan
cháao

receptionist
พนักงานต้อนรับ
pá nák ngaan dtôrn ráp

to check in
เช็กอิน
chék in

room only
เฉพาะห้องพัก
chà pó hông pák

wake-up call
บริการโทรปลุก
bor rí gaan toh bplùk

to check out
เช็กเอาท์
chék áo

full board
รวมอาหารสามมื้อ
ruam aa hăan săam méuu

room number
เบอร์ห้อง
ber hông

to order room service
สั่งอาหารและเครื่อง
ดื่มในห้อง
sàng aa hăan lé krêuang
dèuum nai hông

156

double room
ห้องคู่
hông kôo

key card
คีย์การ์ด/บัตร
กุญแจ
kee gàat/bàt gun jair

minibar
เครื่องดื่มในตู้เย็น
krêuang dèuum nai tôo
yen

porter
พนักงานยกกระเป๋า
pá nák ngaan yók grà
bpǎo

reception
แผนกต้อนรับ
pà nàirk dtôrn ráp

safe
ตู้นิรภัย
dtôo ní rá pai

single room
ห้องเดี่ยว
hông dìaw

toiletries
ของใช้ส่วนตัวในห้องน้ำ
kǒrng chái sùan dtua nai
hông náam

twin room
ห้องเตียงเดี่ยวสำหรับสองคน
hông dtiang dìaw sǎm ràp sǒrng kon

Thailand has a large number of national parks with mountains and waterfalls. Some of them have camping facilities and tents for hire. You can check online to see what guided tours and camping facilities are available.

YOU MIGHT SAY...

Have you got spaces available?
คุณมีที่ว่างอีกไหม
kun mee têe wâang èek mái

I'd like to book for ... nights.
ผม/ฉัน อยากจะจอง ... คืน
pŏm/chán yàak jà jorng ... keuun

How much is it per night?
คืนละเท่าไหร่
keuun lá tâo rài

Where is the toilet/shower block?
ห้องน้ำ/ห้องอาบน้ำอยู่ที่ไหน
hông náam/hông àap náam yòo têe nǎi

Is the water drinkable?
น้ำนี้ดื่มได้ไหม
náam née dèuum dâai mái

YOU MIGHT HEAR...

We have spaces available.
เรายังมีที่ว่าง
rao yang mee têe wâang

We don't have spaces available.
เราไม่มีที่ว่างแล้ว
rao mâi mee têe wâang láew

It costs ... baht per night.
ราคาคืนละ ... บาท
raa kaa keuun lá ... bàat

The toilets/showers are located...
ห้องน้ำ/ห้องอาบน้ำอยู่ที่...
hông náam/hông àap náam yòo têe...

The water is/is not drinkable.
น้ำนี้ดื่มได้/ไม่ได้
náam née dèuum dâai/mâi dâai

VOCABULARY

camper
คนไปแคมป์
kon bpai kairm

campsite
ที่ตั้งแคมป์
têe dtâng kairm

pitch
จุดกางเต็นท์
jùt gaang dtén

electricity hook-up
จุดต่อไฟฟ้า
jùt dtòr fai fáa

toilet/shower block
ห้องน้ำ/ห้องอาบน้ำ
hông náam/hông àap náam

groundsheet
แผ่นรองพื้น
pèn rorng péuun

to camp	to pitch a tent	to take down a tent
ไปแคมป์	กางเต็นท์	เก็บเต็นท์
bpai kairm	gaang dtén	gèp dtén

air bed
ฟูกเป่าลม
fôok bpào lom

camping stove
เตาแก๊สกระป๋อง
dtao gáirt grà bpŏrng

caravan
รถคาราวาน
rót kaa raa waan

cool box
กระติกน้ำแข็ง
grà dtìk náam kĕng

matches
ไม้ขีดไฟ
máai kèet fai

motorhome
รถบ้าน
rót bâan

sleeping bag
ถุงนอน
tŭng norn

tent
เต็นท์
dtén

torch
ไฟฉาย
fai chăai

Thailand has over 3,000 kilometres of coastline, running along the Gulf of Thailand as well as the Andaman Sea. There are rocky cliffs, sandy beaches, and a host of lush tropical islands, all well worth visiting.

YOU MIGHT SAY...

Is there a good beach nearby?
แถวนี้มีหาดสวยๆไหม
tăew née mee hàat sŭay sŭay mái

Is swimming permitted here?
ที่นี่ว่ายน้ำได้ไหม
têe nêe wâai náam dâai mái

Can we hire...?
เราขอเช่า ... ได้ไหม
rao kŏr châo ... dâai mái

Help! Someone is drowning!
ช่วยด้วย! คนจมน้ำ!
chûay dûay! kon jom náam

YOU MIGHT HEAR...

This is a public beach.
นี่เป็นหาดสาธารณะ
nêe bpen hàat săa taa rá ná

Swimming is allowed/forbidden.
ว่ายน้ำได้/ห้ามว่ายน้ำ
wâai náam dâai/hâam wâai náam

Swimming is/is not supervised.
มี/ไม่มีการดูแลคนว่ายน้ำ
mee/mâi mee gaan doo lair kon wâai náam

The water is warm/cold/freezing!
น้ำอุ่น/เย็น/เย็นจัด
náam ùn/yen/yen jàt

YOU SHOULD KNOW...

Thailand is world-famous for its coral reefs. Many of its beaches and islands have diving and kayaking opportunities. However, new measures have been put into effect to try and stop environmental damage from tourism. Check whether any guidelines apply to your planned activities and avoid littering.

VOCABULARY

seaside	"No swimming"	bathing zone
ชายทะเล	ห้ามว่ายน้ำ	เขตว่ายน้ำ
chaai tá lay	hâam wâai náam	kàyt wâai náam

"No sunbathing"
ห้ามอาบแดด
hâam àap dàirt

beach hut
กระท่อมริมหาด
grà tôm rim hàat

to sunbathe
อาบแดด
àap dàirt

lifeguard
เจ้าหน้าที่ช่วยคนตกน้ำ
jâo nâa têe chûay kon
dtòk náam

promenade
ทางเดินเลียบหาด
taang dern lîap hàat

to swim
ว่ายน้ำ
wâai náam

GENERAL

beach ball
ลูกบอลชายหาด
lôok born chaai hàat

beach toys
ของเล่นชายหาด
kŏrng lên chaai hàat

bikini
ชุดบิกินี
chút bì gì nee

deckchair
เก้าอี้ชายหาด
gâo êe chaai hàat

flip-flops
รองเท้าแตะ
rorng táao tè

flippers
ฟิน
fin

hammock
เปล
bplay

sandcastle
ปราสาททราย
bpraa sàat saai

seashells
เปลือกหอย
bplèuak hŏy

seaweed
สาหร่าย
săa ràai

sunglasses
แว่นกันแดด
wên gan dàirt

sunhat
หมวก
mùak

suntan lotion
ครีมกันแดด
kreem gan dàirt

swimming trunks
กางเกงว่ายน้ำ
gaang gayng wâai náam

swimsuit
ชุดว่ายน้ำ
chút wâai náam

THE SEASIDE

beach towel	sand	sea	waves	parasol
ผ้าเช็ดตัวริมหาด	ทราย	ทะเล	คลื่น	ร่มกันแดด
pâa chét dtua rim hàat	saai	tá lay	klêuun	rôm gan dàirt

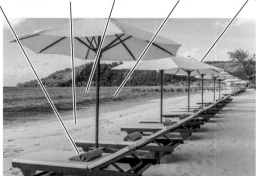

YOU MIGHT SAY...

I enjoy listening to music.
ผม /ฉัน ชอบฟังเพลง
pŏm/chán chôrp fang playng

I'm learning to play...
ผม /ฉัน กำลังหัดเล่น...
pŏm/chán gam lang hàt lên...

What kind of music do you like?
คุณชอบเพลงแบบไหน
kun chôrp playng bàirp năi

YOU MIGHT HEAR...

I like/don't like...
ผม /ฉัน ชอบ/ไม่ชอบ...
pŏm/chán chôrp/mâi chôrp...

My favourite group is...
วงที่ ผม /ฉัน ชอบที่สุดคือ...
wong têe pŏm/chán chôrp têe sùt keuu...

VOCABULARY

song เพลง playng	DJ ดีเจ dee jay	rock เพลงร็อค playng rók
album อัลบั้ม an lá bâm	vinyl record แผ่นเสียง pèn sĭang	classical เพลงคลาสสิก playng klâat sìk
band วง wong	turntable เครื่องเล่นแผ่นเสียง krêuang lên pèn sĭang	folk เพลงโฟล์ค playng fóhk
live music ดนตรีสด don dtree sòt	microphone ไมโครโฟน mai kroh fohn	Thai country music เพลงลูกทุ่ง playng lôok tûng
gig การแสดงสด gaan sà dairng sòt	pop เพลงป๊อป playng bpórp	to play an instrument เล่นเครื่องดนตรี lên krêuang don dtree

to sing	to listen to music	to go to gigs
ร้องเพลง	ฟังเพลง	ไปดูการแสดงสด
rórng playng	fang playng	bpai doo gaan sà dairng sòt

YOU SHOULD KNOW...

Gigs held in open-air restaurants and bars tend to be pop or rock music. If you want to go and see Thai-style country music, known as "lôok tûng", it may be easier with the help of a local.

EQUIPMENT

earphones
หูฟัง
hǒo fang

headphones
หูฟังแบบครอบ
hǒo fang bàirp krôrp

speakers
ลำโพง
lam pohng

MUSICAL INSTRUMENTS

accordion
หีบเพลงชัก
hèep playng chák

acoustic guitar
กีตาร์โปร่ง
gee dtâa bpròhng

bass drum
กลองใหญ่
glorng yài

bass guitar
กีตาร์เบส
gee dtâa bàyt

cello
เชลโล
chayn loh

clarinet
แคลริเน็ท
klair rí nèt

cymbals
ฉาบ
chàap

double bass
ดับเบิลเบส
dàp bern bàyt

drum
กลอง
glorng

electric guitar
กีตาร์ไฟฟ้า
gee dtâa fai fáa

flute
ฟลูต
flóot

harp
ฮาร์ป
háap

keyboard
คีย์บอร์ด
kee bòrt

mouth organ
หีบเพลงปาก
hèep playng bpàak

piano
เปียโน
bpia noh

saxophone
แซกโซโฟน
sék soh fohn

trombone
ทรอมโบน
trorm bohn

trumpet
ทรัมเป็ต
tram bpèt

tuba
ทูบา
too baa

violin
ไวโอลิน
wai oh lin

xylophone
ระนาดฝรั่ง
rá nâat fà ràng

TRADITIONAL THAI INSTRUMENTS

Thai wooden dulcimer
ขิม
kǐm

treble fiddle
ซอ
sor

zither
จะเข้
jà kây

GENERAL MUSIC

choir
คณะประสานเสียง
ká ná bprà sǎan sǐang

conductor
วาทยกร
waa tá yá gorn

musician
นักดนตรี
nák don dtree

orchestra
ออร์เคสตรา
or kàyt dtraa

sheet music
โน้ตดนตรี
nóht don dtree

singer
นักร้อง
nák rórng

YOU MIGHT SAY/HEAR...

Can I take photos here?
ผม/ฉัน ถ่ายรูปที่นี่ได้ไหม
pŏm/chán tàai rôop têe nêe dâai mái

Say cheese!
ยิ้มหน่อย
yím nòy

VOCABULARY

photographer
ช่างถ่ายภาพ
châng tàai pâap

selfie
เซลฟี่
sayn fêe

to take a photo/selfie
ถ่ายรูป/ถ่ายเซลฟี่
tàai rôop/tàai sayn fêe

photo
รูป
rôop

selfie stick
ไม้เซลฟี่
máai sayn fêe

to zoom in
ซูมเข้า
soom kâo

camera lens
เลนส์กล้อง
layn glông

compact camera
กล้องเล็ก
glông lék

drone
โดรน
drohn

DSLR camera
กล้องใหญ่
glông yài

SD card
แผ่นความจำ
pèn kwaam jam

tripod
ขาตั้งกล้อง
kăa dtâng glông

Traditional Thai chess looks similar to European chess but has a slightly different set of rules. Both games are thought to share a common ancestor. Nowadays computer and phone games are very popular with many people.

YOU MIGHT SAY...

Shall we play a game?
เราเล่นเกมกันไหม
rao lên gaym gan mái

What would you like to play?
คุณอยากเล่นอะไร
kun yàak lên à rai

How do you play?
คุณเล่นยังไง
kun lên yang ngai

YOU MIGHT HEAR...

It's your turn.
ตาคุณแล้ว
dtaa kun láew

Time's up!
หมดเวลา
mòt way laa

Shall we play something else?
เราเล่นอย่างอื่นกันไหม
rao lên yàang èuun gan mái

VOCABULARY

player
ผู้เล่น
pôo lên

poker
โป๊กเกอร์
bpóhk gêr

games console
เครื่องเล่นเกม
krêuang lên gaym

game controller
ตัวบังคับเกม
dtua bang káp gaym

video game
วิดีโอเกม
wí dee oh gaym

virtual reality headset
ชุดหน้ากากวีอาร์
chút nâa gàak wee aa

draughts
หมากฮอส
màak hôrt

hand (in cards)
ไพ่ในมือ
pâi nai meuu

to play
เล่น
lên

to roll the dice
โยนลูกเต๋า
yohn lôok dtăo

to win
ชนะ
chá ná

to lose
แพ้
páir

board game
เกมกระดาน
gaym grà daan

bowling
โบว์ลิ่ง
boh lîng

cards
ไพ่
pâi

chess
หมากรุก
màak rúk

crossword
อักษรไขว้
àk sŏrn kwâi

darts
ปาลูกดอก
bpaa lôok dòrk

dice
ลูกเต๋า
lôok dtăo

dominoes
โดมิโน
doh mí noh

go
โกะ
gò

jigsaw puzzle
ภาพต่อจิกซอว์
pâap dtòr jìk sor

mahjong
ไพ่นกกระจอก
pâi nók grà jòrk

Thai chess
หมากรุกไทย
màak rúk tai

169

ARTS AND CRAFTS | ศิลปะและงานฝีมือ

Thailand is home to a wide range of local arts and crafts. The Thai silk industry is particularly famous and tourists are able to purchase a wide range of silk goods. Some of the hill tribes also produce their own unique handicrafts.

VOCABULARY

handicrafts	dressmaker	to sew
งานฝีมือ	ช่างตัดเสื้อ	เย็บ
ngaan fĕe meuu	châng dtàt sêua	yép
artist	to paint	to knit
ศิลปิน	วาด	ถัก
sĭn lá bpin	wâat	tàk
amateur	to sketch	to be creative
มือสมัครเล่น	ร่าง	สร้างสรรค์
meuu sà màk lên	râang	sâang săn

GENERAL CRAFTS

calligraphy
การเขียนตัวอักษร
gaan kĭan dtua àk sŏrn

calligraphy pen
ปากกาคอแร้ง
bpàak gaa kor ráirng

cross-stitch
ปักครอสติช
bpàk krórt sà dtìt

embroidery
งานปัก
ngaan bpàk

jewellery-making
การร้อยเครื่องประดับ
gaan róy krêuang bprà dàp

model-making
การทำแบบจำลอง
gaan tam bàirp jam lorng

papercrafts
งานกระดาษ
ngaan grà dàat

pottery
งานปั้น
ngaan bpân

woodwork
งานไม้
ngaan máai

ART MATERIALS

canvas
ผ้าใบวาดรูป
pâa bai wâat rôop

easel
ขาตั้งวาดรูป
kǎa dtâng wâat rôop

ink
หมึก
mèuk

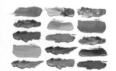
oil paint
สีน้ำมัน
sěe náam man

paintbrush
แปรงวาดรูป
bprairng wâat rôop

palette
จานสี
jaan sěe

pastels
สีชอร์คพาสเทล
sěe chórk pàat tayn

sketchpad
สมุดวาดรูป
sà mùt wâat rôop

watercolours
สีน้ำ
sěe náam

ball of wool
ไหมพรม
măi prom

buttons
กระดุม
grà dum

fabric
ผ้า
pâa

fabric scissors
กรรไกรตัดผ้า
gan grai dtàt pâa

knitting needles
ไม้นิตติ้ง
máai nít dtîng

needle and thread
เข็มกับด้าย
kĕm gàp dâai

safety pin
เข็มกลัดซ่อนปลาย
kĕm glàt sôrn bplaai

sewing machine
จักรเย็บผ้า
jàk yép pâa

tape measure
สายวัด
săai wát

SPORT | กีฬา

As in most other places, sports are popular in Thailand. It is common to see people in the street or in parks kicking "takraw" balls over a net. Thai-style kickboxing, or Muay Thai, has become well-known worldwide as a competitive sport and as a martial art. Football is also a hugely popular spectator sport in Thailand.

football pitch
สนามฟุตบอล
sà năam fút born

centre circle
วงกลมกลางสนาม
wong glom glaang sà năam

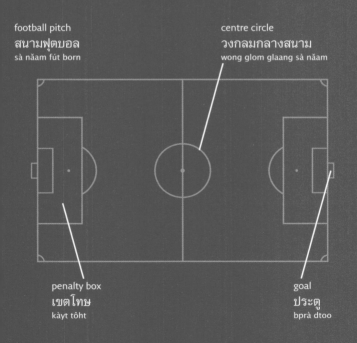

penalty box
เขตโทษ
kàyt tôht

goal
ประตู
bprà dtoo

YOU MIGHT SAY...

I play volleyball/football.
ผม/ฉัน เล่น วอลเลย์บอล/ฟุตบอล
pŏm/chán lên worn lay born/fút born

I'd like to book...
ผม/ฉัน อยากจองตั๋ว...
pŏm/chán yàak jorng dtŭa...

YOU MIGHT HEAR...

Do you do any sports?
คุณเล่นกีฬาไหม
kun lên gee laa mái

What's your favourite team?
คุณชอบทีมอะไรมากที่สุด
kun chôrp teem à rai mâak têe sùt

VOCABULARY

tournament
ทัวร์นาเม้นต์/
การแข่งขัน
tua naa máyn/
gaan kèng kǎn

competition
การแข่งขัน
gaan kèng kǎn

league
ลีค
lèek

champion
แชมเปียน
chairm bpian

competitor
คู่แข่ง
kôo kèng

teammate
เพื่อนร่วมทีม
pêuan rûam teem

sportsperson
นักกีฬา
nák gee laa

coach
โค้ช
kóht

manager
ผู้จัดการ
pôo jàt gaan

match
การแข่งขัน
gaan kèng kǎn

points
คะแนน
ká nairn

locker
ล็อคเกอร์
lók gêr

to coach
ฝึกซ้อม
fèuk sórm

to compete
แข่งขัน
kèng kǎn

to score
ทำคะแนน
tam ká nairn

to win
ชนะ
chá ná

to lose
แพ้
páir

to draw
เสมอกัน
sà měr gan

174

changing room
ห้องเปลี่ยนเสื้อผ้า
hông bplian sêua pâa

leisure centre
ศูนย์กีฬา
sŏon gee laa

medal
เหรียญ
rĭan

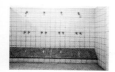

podium
โพเดียม/แท่นรับรางวัล
poh diam/tâirn ráp raang wan

referee
กรรมการ
gam má gaan

scoreboard
ป้ายบอกคะแนน
bpâai bòrk ká nairn

showers
ห้องอาบน้ำ
hông àap náam

spectators
ผู้ชม
pôo chom

stadium
สเตเดียม/สนามกีฬา
sà dtay diam/sà năam gee laa

stands
ที่นั่ง
têe nâng

team
ทีม
teem

trophy
ถ้วยรางวัล
tûay raang wan

Whether you like working out in the gym, taking a fitness class, or just going out for a run, there are many options for you to keep fit in Thailand.

YOU MIGHT SAY...

I'd like to join the gym.
ผม/ฉัน อยากสมัครฟิตเนส
pǒm/chán yàak sà màk fít nâyt

I'd like to book a class.
ผม/ฉัน อยากจะจองคลาส ครับ/ค่ะ
pǒm/chán yàak jorng kláat kráp/kâ

What classes can you do here?
ที่นี่มีคลาสอะไรบ้าง
têe nêe mee kláat à rai bâang

YOU MIGHT HEAR...

Are you a member here?
คุณเป็นสมาชิกที่นี่ใช่ไหม
kun bpen sà maa chík têe nêe châi mái

What time do you want to book for?
คุณอยากจองกี่โมง
kun yàak jorng gèe mohng

We have 12 different classes.
เรามีสิบสองคลาสไม่ซ้ำกัน
rao mee sìp sǒrng kláat mâi sám gan

VOCABULARY

gym
ยิม/ฟิตเนส
yim/fít nâyt

gym instructor
เจ้าหน้าที่ฟิตเนส/
เทรนเนอร์
jâo nâa têe fít nâyt/
trayn ner

gym membership
สมาชิกฟิตเนส
sà maa chík fít nâyt

personal trainer
เทรนเนอร์ส่วนตัว
trayn ner sùan dtua

fitness class
คลาสออกกำลังกาย
kláat òrk gam lang gaai

class timetable
ตารางเวลาคลาส
dtaa raang way laa kláat

running club
ชมรมวิ่ง
chom rom wîng

to keep fit
รักษาความฟิต/
ความแข็งแรง
rák sǎa kwaam fít/kwaam
kěng rairng

to exercise
ออกกำลังกาย
òrk gam lang gaai

to do a fitness class
เข้าคลาสออกกำลัง
กาย
kâo kláat òrk gam lang
gaai

to go for a run
ไปวิ่ง
bpai wîng

to go to the gym
ไปฟิตเนส
bpai fít nâyt

cross trainer
เครื่องสกายวอล์ค/
ครอสเทรนเนอร์
krêuang sà gaai wórk/
krórt trayn nêr

dumbbell
ดัมเบล/เวท
dam bayn/wáyt

exercise bike
จักรยาน
ออกกำลังกาย
jàk grà yaan
òrk gam lang gaai

exercise mat
เสื่อออกกำลังกาย
sèua òrk gam lang gaai

foam roller
โฟมนวดกล้ามเนื้อ
fohm nûat glâam néua

gym ball
ลูกบอลออกกำลังกาย
lôok born òrk gam lang
gaai

hand weights
ดัมเบล
dam bayn

kettle bell
เคตเทิลเบล
káyt têrn bayn

rowing machine
กรรเชียงบก
gan chiang bòk

skipping rope
เชือกกระโดด
chêuak grà dòht

treadmill
เครื่องวิ่ง
krêuang wîng

weightlifting bench
ชุดยกน้ำหนัก
chút yók nám nàk

aerobics
แอโรบิก
air roh bìk

circuit training
เซอร์กิตเทรนนิ่ง
ser gìt trayn nîng

lunges
ลันจ์/ท่าออกกำลัง
ต้นขา
lán/tâa òrk gam lang
dtôn kǎa

Pilates
พิลาทิส
pí laa tít

press-ups
วิดพื้น
wít péuun

running
วิ่ง
wîng

sit-ups
ซิทอัป
sít àp

spinning
การปั่นจักรยาน
gaan bpàn jàk grà yaan

squats
สควอท
sà kwórt

water aerobics
แอโรบิกในน้ำ
air roh bìk nai náam

weightlifting
ยกน้ำหนัก
yók nám nàk

yoga
โยคะ
yoh ká

YOU MIGHT SAY...

I'd like to learn to play table tennis.
ผม/ฉัน อยากหัดเล่นปิงปอง
pŏm/chán yàak hàt lên bping bporng

I know the basic rules.
ผม/ฉัน รู้กติกาพื้นฐาน
pŏm/chán róo gà dtì gaa péuun tăn

How much is each lesson?
ค่าเรียนครั้งละเท่าไหร่
kâa rian kráng lá tâo rài

YOU MIGHT HEAR...

Have you played table tennis before?
คุณเคยเล่นปิงปองไหม
kun koey lên bping bporng mái

We have classes for different levels.
เรามีคลาสหลายระดับ
rao mee kláat lăai rá dàp

Each lesson is 300 baht.
ค่าเรียนครั้งละสามร้อยบาท
kâa rian kráng lá săam róy bàat

VOCABULARY

to play table tennis
เล่นปิงปอง
lên bping bporng

to serve
เสิร์ฟ
sèrp

to receive
รับ
ráp

to smash
ตบ
dtòp

to hit the net
ติดเน็ต
dtit nét

to go off the table
ออกนอกโต๊ะ
òrk nôrk dtó

table tennis bat
ไม้ปิงปอง
máai bping bporng

table tennis net
เน็ตโต๊ะปิงปอง
nét dtó bping bporng

table tennis table
โต๊ะปิงปอง
dtó bping bporng

FOOTBALL | ฟุตบอล

Football is extremely popular in Thailand. Don't be surprised if you find a taxi driver who knows more about the British football leagues than you do! The World Cup is also enjoyed by vast numbers of Thai people. Thai domestic football is shown on television and it is possible to see live matches in stadiums (such as those in Bangkok or Buriram).

YOU MIGHT SAY...

Are you going to watch the match?
คุณจะดูแข่งฟุตบอลไหม
kun jà doo kèng fút born mái

What's the score?
คะแนนเท่าไหร่แล้ว
ká nairn tâo rài láew

That was a foul!
นั้นฟาวล์
nán faao

YOU MIGHT HEAR...

I'm watching the match.
ผม/ฉัน กำลังดูแข่งฟุตบอล
pŏm/chán gam lang doo kèng fút born

The score is...
คะแนน...
ká nairn...

Go on!
ลุยเลย
luy loey

VOCABULARY

defender
กองหลัง
gorng lăng

striker
กองหน้า
gorng nâa

substitute
ตัวสำรอง
dtua săm rorng

kick-off
คิกออฟ
kík órp

half-time
ครึ่งเวลา
krêung way laa

full-time
หมดเวลา
mòt way laa

extra time
ต่อเวลา
dtòr way laa

injury time
ทดเวลาบาดเจ็บ
tót way laa bàat jèp

free kick
ฟรีคิก
free kík

header
การโหม่งลูก
gaan mòhng lôok

save
เซฟ
sáyp

foul
ฟาวล์
faao

offside
ตำแหน่งล้ำหน้า
dtam nèng lám nâa

to play football
เล่นฟุตบอล
lên fút born

to tackle
แย่งลูก
yâirng lôok

penalty
ลูกโทษ
lôok tôht

to kick
เตะ
dtè

to pass the ball
ส่งลูก
sòng lôok

penalty box
เขตโทษ
kàyt tôht

to dribble
เลี้ยงลูก
líang lôok

to score a goal
ทำประตู
tam bprà dtoo

football
ลูกฟุตบอล
lôok fút born

football boots
รองเท้าฟุตบอล
rorng táao fút born

football match
การแข่งฟุตบอล
gaan kèng fút born

football pitch
สนามฟุตบอล
sà nǎam fút born

football player
นักฟุตบอล
nák fút born

goal
โกล์/ประตู
goh/bprà dtoo

goalkeeper
ผู้รักษาประตู
pôo rák sǎa bprà dtoo

whistle
นกหวีด
nók wèet

yellow/red card
ใบเหลือง/ใบแดง
bai lěuang/bai dairng

In addition to table tennis, badminton is also a much-enjoyed sport and has received a lot of media attention ever since Ratchanok Intanon won the women's world championships in 2013.

VOCABULARY

ace
ลูกเสิร์ฟที่ผู้รับไม่
สามารถรับได้
lôok sèrp têe pôo ráp
mâi săa mâat ráp dâai

serve
ลูกเสิร์ฟ
lôok sèrp

backhand
แบ็คแฮนด์
bèk hairn

forehand
โฟร์แฮนด์
foh hairn

fault
การเสิร์ฟเสีย
gaan sèrp sĭa

double fault
การเสิร์ฟลูกเสีย
สองครั้ง
gaan sèrp lôok sĭa
sŏrng kráng

rally
การตีโต้
gaan dtee dtôh

singles
เล่นเดี่ยว
lên dìaw

doubles
เล่นคู่
lên kôo

top seed
มืออันดับท็อป
meuu an dàp tóp

to play tennis
เล่นเทนนิส
lên tayn nít

to play badminton/
squash
เล่นแบดมินตัน/
สควอช
lên bàirt min dtan/
sà kwórt

to hit
ตี
dtee

to serve
เสิร์ฟ
sèrp

to break his/her serve
เอาชนะฝ่ายเสิร์ฟได้
ao chá ná fàai sèrp dâai

BADMINTON

badminton
แบดมินตัน
bàirt min dtan

badminton racket
ไม้แบดมินตัน
máai bàirt min dtan

shuttlecock
ลูกขนไก่/ลูกแบด
lôok kŏn gài/lôok bàirt

ball boy/girl
เด็กเก็บลูก
dèk gèp lôok

line judge
ผู้กำกับเส้น
pôo gam gàp sên

tennis
เทนนิส
tayn nít

tennis ball
ลูกเทนนิส
lôok tayn nít

tennis court
สนามเทนนิส
sà năam tayn nít

tennis player
นักเทนนิส
nák tayn nít

tennis racket
ไม้เทนนิส
máai tayn nít

umpire
ผู้ตัดสิน
pôo dtàt sĭn

umpire's chair
เก้าอี้ผู้ตัดสิน
gâo êe pôo dtàt sĭn

SQUASH

squash
สควอช
sà kwórt

squash ball
ลูกสควอช
lôok sà kwórt

squash racket
ไม้สควอช
máai sà kwórt

183

VOCABULARY

layup
การกระโดดแล้วส่ง
ลูกลงห่วง
gaan grà dòht láew sòng
lôok long hùang

slam dunk
การจับลูกบาสลงห่วง
gaan jàp lôok bàat long
hùang

free throw
การชู้ตลูกโทษ
gaan chóot lôok tôht

to play basketball
เล่นบาสเก็ตบอล
lên bàat gèt born

to catch
รับลูก
ráp lôok

to throw
โยนลูก
yohn lôok

to dribble
เลี้ยงลูก
líang lôok

to block
บล็อก
blòk

to mark a player
กั้น
gân

basket
ห่วง
hùang

basketball
ลูกบาส
lôok bàat

basketball court
สนามบาส
sà năam bàat

basketball game
การแข่งบาสเก็ตบอล
gaan kèng bàat gèt born

basketball player
นักบาสเก็ตบอล
nák bàat gèt born

basketball shoes
รองเท้าบาสเก็ตบอล
rorng táao bàat gèt born

Various forms of water sports can be enjoyed in coastal areas. Snorkelling and scuba diving are popular tourist pursuits, and it is sometimes possible to rent kayaks for the day.

YOU MIGHT SAY...

Can I hire...?
ผม/ฉัน ขอเช่า ... ได้ไหม
pŏm/chán kŏr châo ... dâai mái

I'm a keen swimmer.
ผม/ฉัน ว่ายน้ำเก่ง
pŏm/chán wâai náam gèng

YOU MIGHT HEAR...

You must wear a lifejacket.
คุณต้องใส่เสื้อชูชีพ
kun dtông sài sêua choo chêep

You can hire...
คุณเช่า ... ได้
kun châo ... dâai

VOCABULARY

breaststroke ท่ากบ tâa gòp	swimming lesson เรียนว่ายน้ำ rian wâai náam	to swim ว่ายน้ำ wâai náam
backstroke ท่ากรรเชียง tâa gan chiang	diving การดำน้ำ gaan dam náam	to dive ดำน้ำ dam náam
front crawl ท่าฟรีสไตล์ tâa free sà dtai	diver นักดำน้ำ nák dam náam	to surf โต้คลื่น dtôh klêuun
butterfly ท่าผีเสื้อ tâa pěe sêua	angling ตกปลา dtòk bplaa	to paddle พาย paai
lane ลู่ lôo	angler นักตกปลา nák dtòk bplaa	to row พาย paai
length ความยาว kwaam yaao	surfer นักโต้คลื่น nák dtôh klêuun	to fish ตกปลา dtòk bplaa

armbands
ปลอกแขนว่ายน้ำ
bplòrk kǎirn wâai náam

diving board
สปริงบอร์ด
sà bpring bòrt

goggles
แว่นตาว่ายน้ำ
wâirn dtaa wâai náam

swimmer
นักว่ายน้ำ
nák wâai náam

swimming cap
หมวกว่ายน้ำ
mùak wâai náam

swimming pool
สระว่ายน้ำ
sà wâai náam

swimming trunks
กางเกงว่ายน้ำ
gaang gayng wâai náam

swimsuit
ชุดว่ายน้ำ
chút wâai náam

water polo
โปโลน้ำ
bpoh loh náam

bodyboarding
บอดี้บอร์ด
bor dêe bòrt

canoeing
พายเรือแคนู
paai reua kair noo

jet ski
เจ็ทสกี
jèt sà gee

kayaking
พายเรือคายัค
paai reua kaa yák

lifejacket
เสื้อชูชีพ
sêua choo chêep

oars
ไม้พาย
máai paai

paddle
ไม้พายคายัค
máai paai kaa yák

paddleboarding
กระดานยืนพาย
grà daan yeuun paai

scuba diving
ดำน้ำลึก
dam náam léuk

snorkelling
ดำน้ำตื้น
dam náam dtêuun

surfboard
กระดานโต้คลื่น
grà daan dtôh klêuun

surfing
โต้คลื่น
dtôh klêuun

waterskiing
สกีน้ำ
sà gee náam

wetsuit
ชุดดำน้ำ
chút dam náam

windsurfing
วินด์เซิร์ฟ
win sérp

COMBAT SPORTS | กีฬาการต่อสู้

Thai-style kickboxing, or Muay Thai, is a popular spectator sport in Thailand. It is possible to go and see live bouts in one of the boxing stadiums, where you can also experience the accompanying music and rituals. Learning with a trainer in a Muay Thai gym is a great way to keep fit as well as an effective form of self-defence.

YOU MIGHT SAY...

I'd like to learn some simple Muay Thai moves.

ผม/ฉัน อยากฝึกท่ามวยไทย ง่ายๆ

pŏm/chán yàak fèuk tâa muay tai ngâai ngâai

Where can I find a martial arts teacher?

ผม/ฉัน จะหาครูสอนศิลปะ การต่อสู้ได้ที่ไหน

pŏm/chán jà hăa kroo sŏrn sĭn lá bpà gaan dtòr sôo dâai têe năi

YOU MIGHT HEAR...

That teacher has been practising Muay Thai for over 30 years.

ครูคนนั้นฝึกมวยไทยสามสิบ กว่าปีแล้ว

kroo kon nán fèuk muay tai săam sìp gwàa bpee láew

Muay Thai is a very good form of exercise.

มวยไทยเป็นการออกกำลังกาย ที่ดีมาก

muay tai bpen gaan òrk gam lang gaai têe dee mâak

VOCABULARY

fight
การต่อสู้
gaan dtòr sôo

boxer
นักมวย
nák muay

fighter
นักสู้
nák sôo

opponent
คู่ต่อสู้
kôo dtòr sôo

wrestling
มวยปล้ำ
muay bplâm

fencing
ฟันดาบ
fan dàap

headguard
เครื่องป้องกันศีรษะ
krêuang bpông gan sĕe sà

mouthguard
ฟันยางนักมวย
fan yaang nák muay

to kick
เตะ
dtè

to box	to punch	to spar
ต่อย	ชก	แย็บ
dtòy	chók	yép

to wrestle	to fence	to knock out
ปล้ำ	ฟันดาบ	น็อคเอ้าท์
bplâm	fan dàap	nók áo

BOXING

boxing gloves
นวม
nuam

boxing ring
เวทีมวย
way tee muay

punchbag
กระสอบทราย
grà sòrp saai

COMBAT SPORTS

judo
ยูโด
yoo doh

karate
คาราเต้
kaa raa dtây

kung fu
กังฟู
gang foo

Muay Thai
มวยไทย
muay tai

taekwondo
เทควันโด
tay kwan doh

Tai Chi
ไทชี
tai chee

VOCABULARY

runner
นักวิ่ง
nák wîng

race
การแข่ง
gaan kèng

marathon
วิ่งมาราธอน
wîng maa raa torn

sprint
การวิ่งระยะสั้น
gaan wîng rá yá sân

lane
ลู่
lôo

start/finish line
เส้นออกตัว/เส้นชัย
sên òrk dtua/sên chai

heat
ความร้อน
kwaam rórn

final
รอบสุดท้าย
rôrp sùt táai

starting block
อุปกรณ์ยันเท้าใน
การออกตัววิ่ง
ùp bpà gòrn yan táao nai
gaan òrk dtua wîng

starter's gun
ปืนปล่อยตัวนักกีฬา
bpeuun bplòy dtua nák
gee laa

triple jump
วิ่งกระโดดไกล
wîng grà dòht glai

heptathlon
สัตตกรีฑา
sàt dtà gree taa

decathlon
ทศกรีฑา
tót sà gree taa

to run
วิ่ง
wîng

to race
แข่ง
kèng

to jump
กระโดด
grà dòht

to throw
ขว้าง
kwâang

athlete
นักกรีฑา
nák gree taa

discus
การขว้างจักร
gaan kwâang jàk

high jump
การวิ่งกระโดดสูง
gaan wîng grà dòht sŏong

hurdles
วิ่งข้ามรั้ว
wîng kâam rúa

javelin
พุ่งแหลน
pûng lăirn

long jump
กระโดดไกล
grà dòht glai

pole vault
กระโดดค้ำ
grà dòht kám

relay
วิ่งผลัด
wîng plàt

running track
ลู่วิ่ง
lôo wîng

shot put
ทุ่มน้ำหนัก
tûm nám nàk

spikes
รองเท้าวิ่งแหลม
rorng táao wîng lăirm

stopwatch
นาฬิกาจับเวลา
naa lí gaa jàp way laa

Cycling as a leisure pursuit is not very common in big cities - though bicycles are regularly used as a mode of transport - and there are very few cycle paths. However, group cycles for exercise have been increasing in popularity.

VOCABULARY

cycling shorts
กางเกงขาสั้น
สำหรับขี่จักรยาน
gaang gayng kǎa sân
sǎm ràp kèe jàk grà yaan

rider
คนขี่จักรยาน
kon kèe jàk grà yaan

road/track race
แข่งบน ถนน/
สนามแข่ง
kèng bon tà nǒn/
sà nǎam kèng

time trial
แข่งจับเวลา
kèng jàp way laa

to ride a bike
ขี่จักรยาน
kèe jàk grà yaan

to pedal
ถีบ
tèep

BMX
บีเอ็มเอ็กซ์
bee em ék

helmet
หมวกนิรภัย
mùak ní rá pai

mountain bike
จักรยานเสือภูเขา
jàk grà yaan sěua poo kǎo

road bike
จักรยานถนน
jàk grà yaan tà nǒn

velodrome
สนามขี่จักรยานในร่ม
sà nǎam kèe jàk grà yaan
nai rôm

water bottle
ขวดน้ำ
kùat náam

VOCABULARY

minigolf
มินิกอล์ฟ
mí ní górp

golf course
สนามกอล์ฟ
sà nǎam górp

clubhouse
คลับเฮาส์
kláp háo

caddie
แคดดี้
két dêe

green
กรีน
green

bunker
หลุมทราย
lǔm saai

hole
หลุม
lǔm

handicap
การนับแต้มต่อ
gaan náp dtêm dtòr

hole-in-one
โฮลอินวัน
hohn in wan

over/under par
โอเวอร์/อันเดอร์
พาร์
oh wer/an der paa

to play golf
เล่นกอล์ฟ
lên górp

to tee off
ตีครั้งแรก
dtee kráng râirk

golf bag
ถุงกอล์ฟ
tǔng górp

golf ball
ลูกกอล์ฟ
lôok górp

golf buggy
รถกอล์ฟ
rót górp

golf club
ไม้กอล์ฟ
máai górp

golfer
นักกอล์ฟ
nák górp

tee
ที
tee

archery
ยิงธนู
ying tá noo

baseball
เบสบอล
bàyt born

climbing
ปีนหน้าผาจำลอง
bpeen nâa pǎa jam lorng

equestrian
การขี่ม้า
gaan kèe máa

fishing
ตกปลา
dtòk bplaa

gymnastics
ยิมนาสติก
yim naa sà dtìk

hockey
ฮอกกี้
hók gêe

sepak takraw
ตะกร้อ
dtà grôr

shooting
ยิงปืน
ying bpeuun

skateboarding
สเก็ตบอร์ด
sà gét bòrt

snooker
สนุกเกอร์
sà núk gêr

volleyball
วอลเลย์บอล
worn lay born

It's important to arrange appropriate cover for healthcare during your time in Thailand. Thailand has a good standard of healthcare, and many people from other countries travel to receive treatment in the country's private hospitals. If you are a holidaymaker, ensure you have appropriate travel insurance in place.

first-aid kit
ชุดปฐมพยาบาล
chút bpà tŏm pá yaa baan

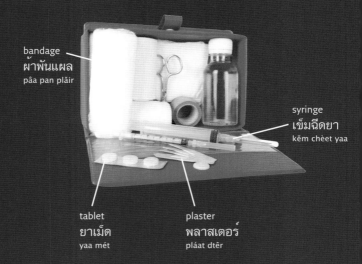

bandage
ผ้าพันแผล
pâa pan plăir

syringe
เข็มฉีดยา
kĕm chèet yaa

tablet
ยาเม็ด
yaa mét

plaster
พลาสเตอร์
pláat dtêr

For minor ailments, the first port of call is normally the pharmacy, which usually has a good stock of common medical supplies. Basics like paracetamol are also available in convenience stores. Foreigners who require medical attention can turn up at hospitals with their passports and will be billed at the end of their hospital visit.

YOU MIGHT SAY...

I don't feel well.
ผม/ฉัน รู้สึกไม่สบาย
pǒm/chán róo sèuk mâi sà baai

I've hurt my...
ผม/ฉัน เจ็บ...
pǒm/chán jèp...

I'm going to be sick.
ผม/ฉัน จะอาเจียน
pǒm/chán jà aa jian

I need to see a doctor.
ผม/ฉัน ต้องหาหมอ
pǒm/chán dtông hǎa mǒr

I need to go to hospital.
ผม/ฉัน ต้องไปโรงพยาบาล
pǒm/chán dtông bpai rohng pá yaa baan

Call an ambulance.
เรียกรถพยาบาล
rîak rót pá yaa baan

YOU MIGHT HEAR...

What's wrong?
เป็นอะไร
bpen à rai

What are your symptoms?
มีอาการอะไรบ้าง
mee aa gaan à rai bâang

Where does it hurt?
เจ็บตรงไหน
jèp dtrong nǎi

How are you today?
วันนี้เป็นยังไง
wan née bpen yang ngai

How long have you been feeling like this?
เป็นแบบนี้กี่วันแล้ว
bpen bàirp née gèe wan láew

VOCABULARY

doctor	nurse	specialist
หมอ/แพทย์	พยาบาล	หมอเฉพาะทาง/
mǒ/pâirt	pá yaa baan	แพทย์เฉพาะทาง
		mǒ chà pó taang

paramedic	pain	health insurance
แพทย์ฉุกเฉิน	ความเจ็บปวด	ประกันสุขภาพ
pâirt chùk chěrn	kwaam jèp bpùat	bprà gan sùk kà pâap
ambulance	illness	healthy
รถฉุกเฉิน	โรค	สุขภาพดี
rót chùk chěrn	rôhk	sùk kà pâap dee
first aid	mental health	to be unwell
ปฐมพยาบาล	สุขภาพจิต	ไม่สบาย
bpà tŏm pá yaa baan	sùk kà pâap jit	mâi sà baai
patient	treatment	to recover
คนไข้	การรักษา	ดีขึ้น
kon kâi	gaan rák săa	dee kêun
medicine	symptom	to look after
ยา	อาการ	ดูแล
yaa	aa gaan	doo lair
painkiller	recovery	to treat
ยาแก้ปวด	การหายดี	รักษา
yaa gâir bpùat	gaan hăai dee	rák săa

If you do end up paying any medical bills, be sure to hold onto the receipts so you can claim through your insurance later.

hospital
โรงพยาบาล
rohng pá yaa baan

pharmacist
เภสัชกร
pay sàt chá gorn

pharmacy
ร้านขายยา
ráan kăai yaa

VOCABULARY

throat	breast	balance
คอ	อก	สมดุล
kor	òk	sŏm dun
eyelash	(body) hair	to see
ขนตา	ขน	เห็น
kŏn dtaa	kŏn	hĕn
eyebrow	height	to smell
คิ้ว	ความสูง	ดมกลิ่น
kíw	kwaam sŏong	dom glìn
eyelid	weight	to hear
เปลือกตา	น้ำหนัก	ได้ยิน
bplèuak dtaa	nám nàk	dâi yin
nostrils	sense of hearing	to touch
รูจมูก	การได้ยิน	จับ
roo jà mòok	gaan dâi yin	jàp
lips	sense of sight	to taste
ริมฝีปาก	การมองเห็น	รับรส
rim fĕe bpàak	gaan morng hĕn	ráp rót
tongue	sense of smell	to stand
ขมับ	การได้กลิ่น	ยืน
kà màp	gaan dâi glìn	yeuun
skin	sense of taste	to walk
ผิวหนัง	การรับรส	เดิน
pĭw năng	gaan ráp rót	dern
genitals	sense of touch	to lose one's balance
อวัยวะเพศ	การสัมผัส	เสียสมดุล
à wai yá wá pâyt	gaan săm pàt	sĭa sŏm dun

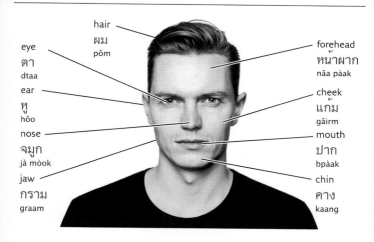

hair
ผม
pŏm

forehead
หน้าผาก
nâa pàak

eye
ตา
dtaa

ear
หู
hŏo

nose
จมูก
jà mòok

jaw
กราม
graam

cheek
แก้ม
gâirm

mouth
ปาก
bpàak

chin
คาง
kaang

HAND

FOOT

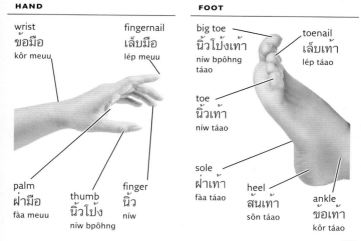

wrist
ข้อมือ
kôr meuu

fingernail
เล็บมือ
lép meuu

palm
ฝ่ามือ
fàa meuu

thumb
นิ้วโป้ง
níw bpôhng

finger
นิ้ว
níw

big toe
นิ้วโป้งเท้า
níw bpôhng
táao

toenail
เล็บเท้า
lép táao

toe
นิ้วเท้า
níw táao

sole
ฝ่าเท้า
fàa táao

heel
ส้นเท้า
sôn táao

ankle
ข้อเท้า
kôr táao

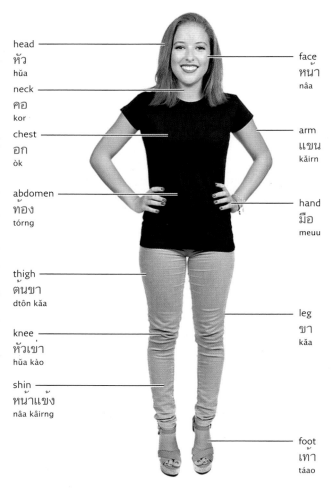

head
หัว
hŭa

neck
คอ
kor

chest
อก
òk

abdomen
ท้อง
tórng

thigh
ต้นขา
dtôn kăa

knee
หัวเข่า
hŭa kào

shin
หน้าแข้ง
nâa kâirng

face
หน้า
nâa

arm
แขน
kăirn

hand
มือ
meuu

leg
ขา
kăa

foot
เท้า
táao

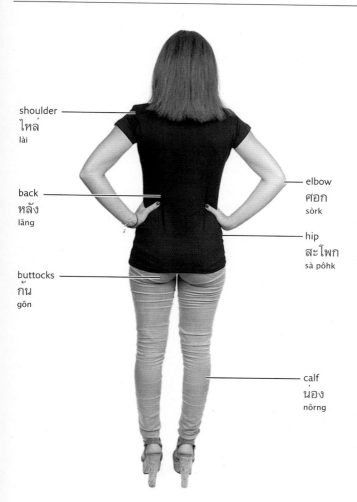

shoulder
ไหล่
lài

back
หลัง
lăng

buttocks
ก้น
gôn

elbow
ศอก
sòrk

hip
สะโพก
sà pôhk

calf
น่อง
nôrng

VOCABULARY

organ	intestines	bone
อวัยวะ	ลำไส้	กระดูก
à wai yá wá	lam sâi	grà dòok
brain	digestive system	skeleton
สมอง	ระบบย่อยอาหาร	โครงกระดูก
sà mŏrng	rá bòb yôy aa hăan	krohng grà dòok
heart	respiratory system	muscle
หัวใจ	ระบบหายใจ	กล้ามเนื้อ
hŭa jai	rá bòp hăai jai	glâam néua
lung	bladder	tendon
ปอด	กระเพาะปัสสาวะ	เส้นเอ็น
bpòrt	grà pó bpàt săa wá	sên en
liver	blood	tissue
ตับ	เลือด	เนื้อเยื่อ
dtàp	lêuat	néua yêua
stomach	oxygen	artery
ท้อง	ออกซิเจน	หลอดเลือดแดง
tórng	òrk sí jayn	lòrt lêuat dairng
kidney	joint	vein
ไต	ข้อต่อ	หลอดเลือดดำ
dtai	kôr dtòr	lòrt lêuat dam

YOU SHOULD KNOW...

Parts of the body feature in several Thai idioms, including:

ก้มหน้าก้มตา (gôm nâa gôm dtaa) meaning: "to concentrate hard on something" (literally: to bow head and eyes)

ขว้างงูไม่พ้นคอ (kwâang ngoo mâi pón kor) meaning: "to do something which turns out to be to one's disadvantage" (literally: to throw a snake no further than one's neck)

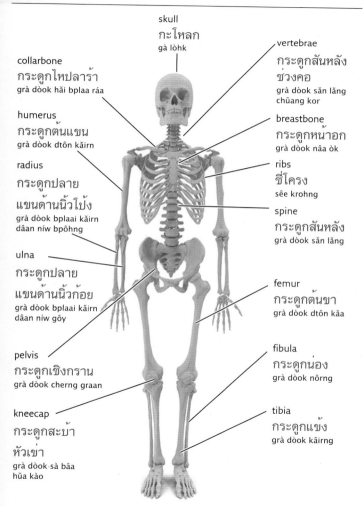

skull
กะโหลก
gà lòhk

vertebrae
กระดูกสันหลัง
ช่วงคอ
grà dòok săn lăng
chûang kor

collarbone
กระดูกไหปลาร้า
grà dòok hăi bplaa rá

humerus
กระดูกต้นแขน
grà dòok dtôn kăirn

breastbone
กระดูกหน้าอก
grà dòok nâa òk

radius
กระดูกปลาย
แขนด้านนิ้วโป้ง
grà dòok bplaai kăirn
dâan níw bpôhng

ribs
ซี่โครง
sêe krohng

spine
กระดูกสันหลัง
grà dòok săn lăng

ulna
กระดูกปลาย
แขนด้านนิ้วก้อย
grà dòok bplaai kăirn
dâan níw gôy

femur
กระดูกต้นขา
grà dòok dtôn kă

pelvis
กระดูกเชิงกราน
grà dòok cherng graan

fibula
กระดูกน่อง
grà dòok nôrng

kneecap
กระดูกสะบ้า
หัวเข่า
grà dòok sà bâa
hŭa kào

tibia
กระดูกแข้ง
grà dòok kâirng

SEEING A DOCTOR | ไปหาหมอ

You can attend a public or private hospital and see a doctor without an appointment. If you do not have a serious health problem and just want a general checkup, it is advisable to go to a private hospital. Doctors in private hospitals can arrange prescriptions for a range of medicines which can be paid for and collected at the end of your appointment.

YOU MIGHT SAY...

I'd like to see a doctor/specialist.
ผม/ฉัน อยากจะพบหมอ/หมอเฉพาะทาง
pŏm/chán yàak jà póp mŏr/mŏr chà pó taang

I need to see a ... specialist.
ผม/ฉัน ขอพบหมอเฉพาะทางด้าน...
pŏm/chán kŏr póp mŏr chà pó taang dâan...

I'm allergic to...
ผม/ฉัน แพ้...
pŏm/chán páir...

I take medication for...
ผม/ฉัน ทานยารักษา...
pŏm/chán taan yaa rák săa...

I've been feeling unwell.
ผม/ฉัน รู้สึกไม่สบาย
pŏm/chán róo sèuk mâi sà baai

YOU MIGHT HEAR...

May I examine you?
ขออนุญาตตรวจนะ ครับ/คะ
kŏr à nú yâat dtrùat ná kráp/ká

Tell me if that hurts.
ถ้าเจ็บบอกนะ ครับ/คะ
tâa jèp bòrk ná kráp/ká

Do you have any allergies?
มีอาการแพ้อะไรไหม
mee aa gaan páir à rai mái

Do you take any medication?
ทานยาอะไรอยู่ไหม
taan yaa à rai yòo mái

You need to see a specialist.
คุณต้องหาหมอเฉพาะทาง
kun dtông hăa mŏr chà pó taang

VOCABULARY

clinic	examination	test
คลินิก	การตรวจ	การตรวจ
klí ník	gaan dtrùat	gaan dtrùat

prescription
ใบสั่งยา
bai sàng yaa

antibiotics
ยาปฏิชีวนะ
yaa bpà dtì chee wá ná

to examine
ตรวจ
dtrùat

vaccination
การฉีดวัคซีน
gaan chèet wák seen

the pill
ยาเม็ด
yaa mét

to be on medication
ทานยารักษา
taan yaa rák săa

medication
ยา
yaa

sleeping pill
ยานอนหลับ
yaa norn làp

to be allergic to...
แพ้...
páir...

blood pressure monitor
เครื่องวัดความดันเลือด
krêuang wát kwaam dan lêuat

examination room
ห้องตรวจ
hông dtrùat

examination table
เตียงตรวจคนไข้
dtiang dtrùat kon kâi

GP
แพทย์ทั่วไป
pâirt tûa bpai

nurse
พยาบาล
pá yaa baan

stethoscope
หูฟังของหมอ
hŏo fang kŏrng mŏr

syringe
หลอดฉีดยา
lòrt chèet yaa

thermometer
ปรอทวัดไข้
bpà ròrt wát kâi

waiting room
ห้องนั่งรอ
hông nâng ror

YOU MIGHT SAY...

Can I book an appointment?
ขอนัดเวลาได้ไหม
kŏr nát way laa dâai mái

I have toothache/an abscess.
ผม/ฉัน ปวดฟัน/เหงือกเป็นหนอง
pŏm/chán bpùat fan/ngèuak bpen nŏrng

My filling has come out.
ฟันที่อุดไว้หลุด
fan têe ùt wái lùt

I've broken my tooth.
ผม/ฉัน ฟันหัก
pŏm/chán fan hàk

YOU MIGHT HEAR...

We don't have any appointments.
เราไม่มีคิวว่าง
rao mâi mee kiw wâang

You need a new filling.
คุณต้องอุดฟันใหม่
kun dtông ùt fan mài

Your tooth has to come out.
ต้องถอนฟัน
dtông tŏrn fan

You need your teeth cleaned.
คุณต้องขูดหินปูนทำความสะอาดฟัน
kun dtông kòot hĭn bpoon tam kwaam sà àat fan

VOCABULARY

molar ฟันกราม fan graam	filling อุดฟัน ùt fan	abscess เหงือกเป็นหนอง ngèuak bpen nŏrng
incisor ฟันหน้า fan nâa	crown ครอบฟัน krôrp fan	extraction การถอนฟัน gaan tŏrn fan
canine ฟันเขี้ยว fan kîaw	root canal treatment การรักษารากฟัน gaan rák săa râak fan	to brush one's teeth แปรงฟัน bprairng fan
wisdom teeth ฟันคุด fan kút	toothache ปวดฟัน bpùat fan	to floss ใช้ไหมขัดฟัน chái măi kàt fan

braces
เหล็กจัดฟัน
lèk jàt fan

dental floss
ไหมขัดฟัน
mǎi kàt fan

dental nurse
พยาบาลทันตกรรม
pá yaa baan tan dtà gam

dentist
หมอฟัน/ทันตแพทย์
mǒr fan/tan dtà pâirt

dentist's chair
เก้าอี้ทำฟัน
gâo êe tam fan

dentist's drill
เครื่องกรอฟัน
krêuang gror fan

dentures
ฟันปลอม
fan bplorm

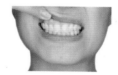

gums
เหงือก
ngèuak

mouthwash
น้ำยาบ้วนปาก
nám yaa bûan bpàak

teeth
ฟัน
fan

toothbrush
แปรงสีฟัน
bprairng sěe fan

toothpaste
ยาสีฟัน
yaa sěe fan

THE OPTICIAN'S | ร้านแว่นตา

Opticians are commercial businesses in Thailand. If you want a pair of glasses, you go directly to the optician's. However, if you have a problem with your eyes, you need to go to the hospital and see an ophthalmologist.

YOU MIGHT SAY...

My eyes are dry/sore.
ตาของ ผม/ฉัน แห้ง/ปวด
dtaa kŏrng pŏm/chán hâirng/bpùat

Do you repair glasses?
คุณซ่อมแว่นไหม
kun sôrm wâirn mái

YOU MIGHT HEAR...

Look up/down/ahead.
มองขึ้น/มองลง/มองตรง
morng kêun/morng long/morng dtrong

You need reading glasses.
คุณต้องใช้แว่นอ่านหนังสือ
kun dtông chái wâirn àan nang sěuu

VOCABULARY

ophthalmologist
จักษุแพทย์
jàk sù pâirt

reading glasses
แว่นอ่านหนังสือ
wâirn àan nang sěuu

bifocals
แว่นสองระยะ
wâirn sŏrng rá yá

lens
เลนส์
layn

conjunctivitis
โรคตาแดง
rôhk dtaa dairng

stye
ตากุ้งยิง
dtaa gûng ying

blurred vision
มองเห็นไม่ชัด
morng hěn mâi chát

cataracts
ต้อกระจก
dtôr grà jòk

short-sighted
สายตาสั้น
săi dtaa sân

long-sighted
สายตายาว
săi dtaa yaao

visually impaired
ความบกพร่องทาง
สายตา
kwaam bòk prông taang
săi dtaa

blind
ตาบอด
dtaa bòrt

colour-blind
ตาบอดสี
dtaa bòrt sěe

to wear glasses
ใส่แว่นตา
sài wâirn dtaa

to use contacts
ใช้คอนแทคเลนส์
chái korn táirk layn

contact lens case
ตลับคอนแทคเลนส์
dtà làp korn táirk layn

contact lenses
คอนแทคเลนส์
korn táirk layn

eye chart
ชาร์ตวัดสายตา
cháat wát sǎai dtaa

eye drops
ยาหยอดตา
yaa yòrt dtaa

eye test
วัดสายตา
wát sǎai dtaa

frames
กรอบแว่น
gròrp wâirn

glasses
แว่นตา
wâirn dtaa

glasses case
กล่องใส่แว่น
glòrng sài wâirn

optician's
ร้านแว่นตา
ráan wâirn dtaa

There are both public and private hospitals in Thailand. Private hospitals cost more but offer greater comfort. Standards are among the highest in the region and private healthcare in Thailand is often accessed by patients from other countries.

YOU MIGHT SAY...

Which ward is ... in?
คุณ ... อยู่แผนกไหน
kun ... yòo pà nàirk nǎi

What are the visiting hours?
เยี่ยมได้กี่โมง
yîam dâai gèe mohng

YOU MIGHT HEAR...

He/She is in ward...
เขาอยู่แผนก...
káo yòo pà nàirk...

Visiting hours are...
เยี่ยมไข้เวลา...
yîam kâi way laa...

VOCABULARY

public hospital
โรงพยาบาลรัฐ
rohng pá yaa baan rát

private hospital
โรงพยาบาลเอกชน
rohng pá yaa baan àyk gà chon

A&E
อุบัติเหตุและฉุกเฉิน
ù bàt dtì hàyt lé chùk chěrn

physiotherapist
นักกายภาพบำบัด
nák gaai yá pâap bam bàt

radiographer
นักรังสีการแพทย์
nák rang sěe gaan pâirt

surgeon
หมอผ่าตัด
mǒr pàa dtàt

operation
ผ่าตัด
pàa dtàt

scan
สแกน
sà gairn

intensive care
การดูแลผู้ป่วยหนัก
gaan doo lair pôo bpùay nàk

diagnosis
วินิจฉัย
wí nít chǎi

defibrillator
เครื่องกระตุกหัวใจไฟฟ้า
krêuang grà dtùk hǔa jai fai fáa

to take his/her pulse
วัดชีพจร
wát chêep pá jorn

to undergo surgery
เข้ารับการผ่าตัด
kâo ráp gaan pàa dtàt

to be admitted/discharged
นอนโรงพยาบาล/ให้กลับบ้าน
norn rohng pá yaa baan/hâi glàp bâan

crutches
ไม้ค้ำ
máai kám

drip
ให้น้ำเกลือ
hâi nám gleua

hospital bed
เตียงโรงพยาบาล
dtiang rohng pá yaa baan

monitor
จอสัญญาณชีพ
jor săn yaan chêep

neck brace
เฝือกอ่อนพยุงคอ
fèuak òrn pá yung kor

operating theatre
ห้องผ่าตัด
hông pàa dtàt

oxygen mask
หน้ากากออกซิเจน
nâa gàak òrk sí jayn

plaster cast
เฝือกแข็ง
fèuak kĕng

ward
แผนก
pà nàirk

wheelchair
เก้าอี้รถเข็น
gâo êe rót kĕn

X-ray
เอ็กซ์-เรย์
ék ray

Zimmer frame®
อุปกรณ์ช่วยเดิน
ùp bpà gorn chûay dern

YOU MIGHT SAY...

Can you help me?
คุณช่วย ผม/ฉัน ได้ไหม
kun chûay pǒm/chán dâai mái

Can you call an ambulance?
ช่วยโทรเรียกรถฉุกเฉินได้ไหม
chûay toh rîak rót chùk chěrn dâai mái

I've had an accident.
ผม/ฉัน มีอุบัติเหตุ
pǒm/chán mee ù bàt dtì hàyt

I've hurt my...
ผม/ฉัน ... เจ็บ
pǒm/chán ... jèp

I've broken my...
ผม/ฉัน ... หัก
pǒm/chán ... hàk

I've sprained my...
ผม/ฉัน ... เคล็ด
pǒm/chán ... klét

I've cut/burnt myself.
ผม/ฉัน มีดบาด/น้ำร้อนลวก
pǒm/chán mêet bàat/nám rórn lûak

I've hit my head.
ผม/ฉัน หัวชน
pǒm/chán hǔa chon

YOU MIGHT HEAR...

Do you feel faint?
คุณจะเป็นลมหรือ
kun jà bpen lom rěr

Do you feel sick?
คุณจะอาเจียนหรือ
kun jà aa jian rěr

I'm calling an ambulance.
ผม/ฉัน จะเรียกรถฉุกเฉิน
pǒm/chán jà rîak rót chùk chěrn

Where does it hurt?
เจ็บตรงไหน
jèp dtrong nǎi

VOCABULARY

concussion	dislocation	scar
สมองกระทบกระเทือน	ข้อเคลื่อน	แผลเป็น
sà mǒrng grà tóp grà teuan	kôr klêuan	plǎir bpen
accident	sprain	swelling
อุบัติเหตุ	เคล็ด	บวม
ù bàt dtì hàyt	klét	buam

recovery position

ท่าพักฟื้น

tâa pák féuun

CPR

การช่วยฟื้นคืนชีพ

gaan chûay féuun keuun chêep

stitches

เย็บ

yép

whiplash

กล้ามเนื้อต้นคอบาดเจ็บ

glâam néua dtôn kor bàat jèp

to injure oneself

ทำตัวเองบาดเจ็บ

tam dtua ayng bàat jèp

to be unconscious

หมดสติ

mòt sà dtì

to fall

ตก

dtòk

to break one's arm

แขนหัก

kǎirn hàk

to twist one's ankle

ข้อเท้าพลิก

kôr táao plík

YOU SHOULD KNOW...

The major phone numbers for emergency services in Thailand are: 1699 or 1669 for medical emergencies (1646 or 1554 in Bangkok); 911 or 191 for general emergencies; 1146 for traffic accidents; and 1155 for English-speaking tourist police.

INJURIES

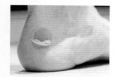

blister

พอง

porng

bruise

ช้ำ

chám

burn

ลวก

lûak

cut

บาด

bàat

fracture

กระดูกหัก

grà dòok hàk

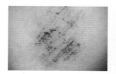

graze

ถลอก

tà lòrk

splinter
เสี้ยนตำ
sîan dtam

sting
แมลงต่อย
má lairng dtòy

sunburn
แพ้แดด
páir dàirt

adhesive tape
เทปกาวทำแผล
táyp gaao tam plăir

bandage
ผ้าพันแผล
pâa pan plăir

dressing
ผ้าก๊อซ
pâa górt

first-aid kit
ชุดปฐมพยาบาล
chút bpà tŏm pá yaa
baan

ice pack
ถุงประคบเย็น
tŭng bprà kóp yen

ointment
ยาขี้ผึ้ง
yaa kêe pêung

plaster
พลาสเตอร์
pláat dter

sling
ผ้าคล้องแขน
pâa klórng kăirn

tweezers
แหนบ
nàirp

YOU MIGHT SAY...

I have the cold/flu.
ผม/ฉัน เป็น หวัด/ไข้หวัดใหญ่
pŏm/chán bpen wàt/kâi wàt yài

I have a sore stomach/a rash/a fever.
ผม/ฉัน ปวดท้อง/เป็นผื่น/มีไข้
pŏm/chán bpùat tórng/bpen pèuun/
mee kâi

I feel faint.
ผม/ฉัน จะเป็นลม
pŏm/chán jà bpen lom

I'm going to be sick.
ผม/ฉัน จะอาเจียน
pŏm/chán jà aa jian

YOU MIGHT HEAR...

You should go to the pharmacy/doctor.
คุณควรไป ร้านขายยา/หาหมอ
kun kuan bpai ráan kăai yaa/hăa mŏr

You need to rest.
คุณต้องพักผ่อน
kun dtông pák pòrn

Do you need anything?
คุณต้องการอะไรไหม
kun dtông gaan à rai mái

Take care of yourself.
ดูแลตัวเองนะ
doo lair dtua ayng ná

VOCABULARY

heart attack
หัวใจวาย
hŭa jai waai

stroke
โรคหลอดเลือดสมอง
rôhk lòrt lêuat sà mŏrng

infection
อักเสบ
àk sàyp

ear infection
หูอักเสบ
hŏo àk sàyp

virus
ไวรัส
wai rát

cold
หวัด
wàt

flu
ไข้หวัดใหญ่
kâi wàt yài

chicken pox
โรคสุกใส
rôhk sùk săi

stomach bug
ท้องเสีย
tórng sĭa

food poisoning
อาหารเป็นพิษ
aa hăan bpen pít

vomiting
อาเจียน
aa jian

diarrhoea
ท้องเสีย
tórng sĭa

constipation	dizziness	to cough
ท้องผูก	เวียนหัว	ไอ
tórng pòok	wian hǔa	ai

diabetes	period pain	to sneeze
เบาหวาน	ปวดประจำเดือน	จาม
bao wǎan	bpùat bprà jam deuan	jaam

epilepsy	inhaler	to vomit
โรคลมชัก	ยาสูดพ่น	อาเจียน
rôhk lom chák	yaa sòot pôn	aa jian

asthma	to have high/low blood pressure	to faint
โรคหอบหืด	มีความดันเลือดสูง/ต่ำ	เป็นลม
rôhk hòrp hèuut	mee kwaam dan lêuat sǒong/dtàm	bpen lom

GENERAL

coughing
ไอ
ai

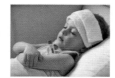

fever
ไข้
kâi

nausea
อาเจียน
aa jian

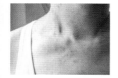

rash
ผื่น
pèuun

runny nose
น้ำมูกไหล
nám môok lǎi

sneezing
จาม
jaam

If you are travelling to or in Thailand while pregnant, make sure you have appropriate travel insurance in place.

YOU MIGHT SAY...

I'm (six months) pregnant.
ฉันท้อง (หกเดือน)
chán tórng hòk deuan

My partner/wife is pregnant.
แฟน/ภรรยา ของผมท้อง
fairn/pan rá yaa kŏrng pŏm tórng

I'm/She's having contractions every ... minutes.
ฉัน/เธอ เจ็บท้องทุก ... นาที
chán/ter jèp tórng túk ... naa tee

My/Her waters have broken.
ฉัน/เธอ น้ำเดินแล้ว
chán/ter náam dern láew

I need pain relief.
ฉันขอยาแก้ปวด
chán kŏr yaa gâir bpùat

YOU MIGHT HEAR...

How far along are you?
ท้องกี่เดือน
tórng gèe deuan

How long is it between contractions?
อาการเจ็บท้องห่างกันกี่นาที
aa gaan jèp tórng hàang gan gèe naa tee

Push!
เบ่ง!
bèng

Do you mind if I examine you?
ขอตรวจดูหน่อยนะครับ/คะ
kŏr dtrùat doo nòy ná kráp/ká

VOCABULARY

pregnant woman
ผู้หญิงท้อง/สตรีมีครรภ์
pôo yǐng tórng/sà dtree mee kan

foetus
ทารกในครรภ์/ลูกใน
ท้อง
taa rók nai kan/lôok nai tórng

uterus
มดลูก
mót lôok

cervix
ปากมดลูก
bpàak mót lôok

labour
เจ็บท้อง
jèp tórng

epidural
บล็อกหลัง
blòk lǎng

Caesarean section
ผ่าคลอด
pàa klôrt

delivery
การคลอด
gaan klôrt

newborn
ทารกแรกเกิด
taa rók râirk gèrt

miscarriage
แท้งลูก
táirng lôok

stillborn
ทารกที่เสียชีวิต
ในครรภ์
taa rók têe sǐa chee wít
nai kan

due date
กำหนดคลอด
gam nòt klôrt

morning sickness
แพ้ท้อง
páir tórng

to fall pregnant
ตั้งครรภ์
dtâng kan

to be in labour
จะคลอด
jà klôrt

to give birth
คลอด
klôrt

to miscarry
แท้งลูก
táirng lôok

to breast-feed
ให้นมลูก
hâi nom lôok

incubator
ตู้อบทารก
dtôo òp taa rók

labour suite
ห้องคลอด
hông klôrt

midwife
พยาบาลผดุงครรภ์
pá yaa baan pà dung kan
zhù chǎn shì

pregnancy test
ตรวจการตั้งครรภ์
dtrùat gaan dtâng kan

sonographer
ผู้เชี่ยวชาญด้าน
อัลตราซาวด์
pôo chîaw chaan dâan an
dtraa saao

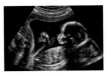

ultrasound
อัลตราซาวด์
an dtraa saao

Traditional Thai massage is world-famous and widely practised to this day. Some tourists go to Thailand for health spas, retreats, and courses in massage or meditation.

VOCABULARY

therapist
นักบำบัด
nák bam bàt

chiropractor
นักไคโรแพรคติก
nák kai roh prék dtìk

to relax
ผ่อนคลาย
pòrn klaai

masseur
หมอนวด
mŏr nûat

acupuncturist
หมอฝังเข็ม
mŏr făng kĕm

to massage
นวด
nûat

masseuse
หมอนวดหญิง
mŏr nûat yĭng

reflexologist
หมอนวดเท้า
mŏr nûat táao

to meditate
นั่งสมาธิ
nâng sà maa tí

YOU SHOULD KNOW...

Massage shops can be found everywhere and are very popular with tourists. If you are finding the pressure of a massage to be too firm, you can say "เบาๆ หน่อย" (bao bao nòy) which means "gently please".

GENERAL

essential oil
น้ำมันหอมระเหย
nám man hŏrm rá hŏey

herbal medicine
ยาสมุนไพร
yaa sà mŭn prai

homeopathy
โฮมิโอพาธี
hoh mí oh paa tee

acupuncture
ฝังเข็ม
fǎng kěm

chiropractic
จัดกระดูก
jàt grà dòok

hypnotherapy
การสะกดจิตบำบัด
gaan sà gòt jìt bam bàt

massage
นวด
nûat

meditation
การฝึกสมาธิ
gaan fèuk sà maa tí

moxibustion
การรมยา
gaan rom yaa

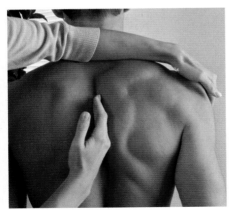

reflexology
นวดเท้า
nûat táao

osteopathy
การรักษาโรคกระดูก
gaan rák sǎa rôhk grà dòok

thalassotherapy
การบำบัดด้วยน้ำทะเล
gaan bam bàt dûay náam
tá lay

If you want to bring your pet to Thailand from the UK, you will need to have a valid health certificate and fill out an application form to get an Import Permit for your pet. You will also have to show that your pet comes from a place where disease is under control, and that it has been vaccinated against major contagious diseases.

YOU MIGHT SAY...

My dog has been hurt.
หมาของ ผม/ฉัน บาดเจ็บ
mǎa kǒrng pǒm/chán bàat jèp

My cat has been sick.
แมวของ ผม/ฉัน ป่วย
maew kǒrng pǒm/chán bpùay

He/She keeps scratching.
มันเกาไม่หยุด
man gao mâi yùt

My dog needs a tapeworm treatment.
หมาของ ผม/ฉัน ต้องถ่าย พยาธิตัวตืด
mǎa kǒrng pǒm/chán dtôrng tàai pá yaa tí dtua dtèuut

YOU MIGHT HEAR...

Can you tell me what the problem is?
บอกได้ไหม ครับ/คะ ว่าเป็น อะไร
bòrk dâai mái kráp/ká wâa bpen à rai

Has your dog been registered?
หมาของคุณขึ้นทะเบียนรึยัง
mǎa kǒrng kun kêun tá bian réu yang

Do you have a rabies vaccination certificate?
คุณมีใบรับรองการฉีดวัคซีนพิษ สุนัขบ้าไหม
kun mee bai ráp rorng gaan chèet wák seen pít sù nák bâa mái

Is he/she eating normally?
กินอาหารได้ปกติไหม
gin aa hǎan dâai bpòk gà dtì mái

YOU SHOULD KNOW...

Veterinary care in major cities is of a high standard, and in most surgeries in urban areas, there will be staff who speak at least basic English. If you are in a more rural area, however, you will probably have to travel to the nearest town or city if you need anything more than routine care, such as vaccinations.

VOCABULARY

veterinary clinic	rabies vaccination	to vaccinate
คลินิกรักษาสัตว์	วัคซีนพิษสุนัขบ้า	ฉีดวัคซีน
klí ník rák sǎa sàt	wák seen pít sù nák bâa	chèet wák seen
pet	pet passport	to worm
สัตว์เลี้ยง	พาสปอร์ตสัตว์เลี้ยง	ถ่ายพยาธิ
sàt líang	páat bpòrt sàt líang	tàai pá yaa tí
flea	quarantine	to spay/neuter
หมัด	กักตัว	ทำหมัน
màt	gàk dtua	tam mǎn
tick	microchip	to put down
เห็บ	ไมโครชิพ	การุณยฆาต
hèp	mai kroh chíp	gaa run yá kâat

GENERAL

collar
ปลอกคอ
bplòrk kor

E-collar
ปลอกคอกันเลีย
bplòrk kor gan lia

lead
เชือกจูง
chêuak joong

muzzle
ตะกร้อครอบปาก
dtà grôr krôrp bpàak

pet carrier
กล่องใส่สัตว์เลี้ยง
glòrng sài sàt líang

vet
สัตวแพทย์
sàt dtà wá pâirt

With its palm tree-lined tropical beaches, coral-laden shores, mountains, waterfalls, and wildlife-rich national parks, Thailand is a great place to explore the beauty and diversity of nature. You will have to pay an entry fee when visiting national parks, which is used to help pay for their maintenance. Some national parks have an abundance of animals and some can be explored with a tour guide. As well as wildlife-watching, tours and treks may offer the chance of some outdoor swimming or cave exploration.

parrot
นกแก้ว
nók gâew

beak
จะงอยปาก
jà ngoy bpàak

tail
หาง
hăang

claw
กรงเล็บ
grong lép

YOU MIGHT SAY/HEAR...

What is the scenery like?
วิวทิวทัศน์เป็นยังไง
wiw tiw tát bpen yang ngai

I'd recommend visiting...
ผม/ฉัน อยากจะแนะนำให้คุณ
ไปเที่ยวที่...
pǒm/chán yàak jà né nam hâi kun
bpai tîaw têe...

VOCABULARY

nature reserve
เขตอนุรักษ์ธรรมชาติ
kàyt à nú rák tam má
châat

zoo
สวนสัตว์
sǔan sàt

animal
สัตว์
sàt

species
สายพันธุ์
sǎai pan

fur
ขนสัตว์
kǒn sàt

wool
ขนสัตว์
kǒn sàt

paw
ฝ่าเท้า
fàa táao

hoof
กีบ
gèep

snout
จมูกสัตว์
jà mòok sàt

mane
แผงคอ
pǎirng kor

tail
หาง
hǎang

claw
กรงเล็บ
grong lép

horn
เขา
kǎo

feather
ขนสัตว์ปีก
kǒn sàt bpèek

wing
ปีก
bpèek

beak
จะงอยปาก
jà ngoy bpàak

warm-blooded
เลือดอุ่น
lêuat ùn

cold-blooded
เลือดเย็น
lêuat yen

to bark
เห่า
hào

to purr
ครางอย่างแมว
kraang yàang maew

to growl
คำราม
kam raam

224

DOMESTIC ANIMALS AND BIRDS
สัตว์เลี้ยงและนกเลี้ยง

Dogs, cats, fish, and birds are popular pets in Thailand.

YOU MIGHT SAY...

Do you have any pets?
คุณมีสัตว์เลี้ยงไหม
kun mee sàt líang mái

Is it OK to bring my pet?
พาสัตว์เลี้ยงไปด้วยได้ไหม
paa sàt líang bpai dûay dâai mái

This is my guide/assistance dog.
นี่คือ สุนัขนำทาง/สุนัขผู้ช่วย
ของ ผม/ฉัน
nêe keuu sù nák nam taang/sù nák
pôo chûay kŏrng pŏm/chán

What's the number for the vet?
สัตวแพทย์เบอร์โทรอะไร
sàt dtà wà pâirt ber toh à rai

YOU MIGHT HEAR...

I have/don't have a pet.
ผม/ฉัน มี/ไม่มี สัตว์เลี้ยง
pŏm/chán mee/mâi mee sàt líang

I'm allergic to pet hair.
ผม/ฉัน แพ้ขนสัตว์เลี้ยง
pŏm/chán páir kŏn sàt líang

Animals are/are not allowed.
อนุญาต/ไม่อนุญาต ให้สัตว์เข้า
à nú yâat/mâi à nú yâat hâi sàt kâo

The phone number for the vet is...
เบอร์โทรของสัตวแพทย์คือ...
ber toh kŏrng sàt dtà wà pâirt keuu...

"Beware of the dog".
ระวังสุนัขดุ
rá wang sù nák dù

YOU SHOULD KNOW...

You may notice the many stray dogs roaming the streets. Should you wish, you can make a donation to foundations or dog shelters dedicated to their care.

VOCABULARY

fish food
อาหารปลา
aa hăan bplaa

cat litter
ทรายแมว
saai maew

farmer
เกษตรกร
gà sàyt dtrà gorn

farm
ฟาร์ม
faam

farmland
พื้นที่การเกษตร
péuun têe gaan gà sàyt

pony
ลูกม้า
lôok máa

bull
กระทิง
grà ting

Siamese cat
แมวสยาม
maew sà yǎam

guide dog
สุนัข/หมา นำทาง
sù nák/mǎa nam taang

flock
ฝูง
fǒong

herd
ฝูงสัตว์บก
fǒong sàt bòk

animal feed
อาหารสัตว์
aa hǎan sàt

hay
ฟาง
faang

straw
ฟาง
faang

to have a pet
เลี้ยงสัตว์
líang sàt

to walk the dog
พาหมาไปเดิน
paa mǎa bpai dern

to go to the vet
ไปหาสัตแพทย์
bpai hǎa sàt dtà wà pâirt

to farm
ทำการเกษตร
tam gaan gà sàyt

budgerigar
นกหงส์หยก
nók hǒng yòk

bulbul
นกปรอดหัวโขน/
นกกรงหัวจุก
nók bpròrt hǔa kǒhn/nók
grong hǔa jùk

cat
แมว
maew

dog
หมา/สุนัข
mǎa/sù nák

goldfish
ปลาทอง
bplaa torng

guinea pig
แกสปี้
gét sà bêe

hamster
แฮมสเตอร์
hairm sà dtêr

horse
ม้า
máa

mynah bird
นกขุนทอง
nók kŭn torng

parrot
นกแก้ว
nók gâew

rabbit
กระต่าย
grà dtàai

rat
หนู
nŏo

FARM ANIMALS

bull
กระทิง
grà ting

chicken
ไก่
gài

cow
วัว
wua

duck
เป็ด
bpèt

goat
แพะ
pé

goose
ห่าน
hàan

pig
หมู
mŏo

sheep
แกะ
gè

water buffalo
ควาย
kwaai

BABY ANIMALS

calf
ลูกวัว
lôok wua

cub
ลูกสัตว์
lôok sàt

fawn
ลูกกวาง
lôok gwaang

foal
ลูกม้า
lôok máa

kid
ลูกแพะ
lôok pé

kitten
ลูกแมว
lôok maew

lamb
ลูกแกะ
lôok gè

piglet
ลูกหมู
lôok mŏo

puppy
ลูกหมา
lôok măa

aquarium
ตู้ปลา
dtôo bplaa

barn
โรงนา
rohng naa

birdcage
กรงนก
grong nók

cage
กรง
grong

dog basket
ที่นอนหมา
têe norn măa

hutch
บ้านกระต่าย
bâan grà dtàai

kennel
บ้านสุนัข
bâan sù nák

litter tray
ถาดทราย
tàat saai

pet bowl
ชามอาหารสัตว์
chaam aa hăan sàt

pet food
อาหารสัตว์
aa hăan sàt

stable
คอกสัตว์
kôrk sàt

trough
รางน้ำของสัตว์
raang náam kŏrng sàt

badger
แบดเจอร์
bét jêr

bat
ค้างคาว
káang kaao

boar
หมูป่า
mǒo bpàa

deer
กวาง
gwaang

fox
หมาจิ้งจอก
mǎa jîng jòrk

gibbon
ชะนี
chá nee

hare
กระต่ายป่า
grà dtàai bpàa

mole
ตุ่น
dtùn

mouse
หนู
nǒo

otter
นาก
nâak

slow loris
ลิงลม
ling lom

squirrel
กระรอก
grà rôrk

OTHER COMMON MAMMALS

bear
หมี
měe

camel
อูฐ
òot

chimpanzee
ชิมแปนซี
chim bpairn see

elephant
ช้าง
cháang

giant panda
แพนด้า
pairn dâa

giraffe
ยีราฟ
yee ráap

hippopotamus
ฮิปโป
híp bpoh

kangaroo
จิงโจ้
jing jôh

lion
สิงโต
sǐng dtoh

monkey
ลิง
ling

rhinoceros
แรด
râirt

tiger
เสือ
sěua

buzzard
เหยี่ยว
yìaw

crane
นกกระเรียนมงกุฎแดง
nók grà rian mong gùt
dairng

crow
กา
gaa

dove
พิราบขาว
pí râap kăao

eagle
นกอินทรี
nók in see

flamingo
นกฟลามิงโก
nók flaa ming goh

gull
นกนางนวล
nók naang nuan

heron
นกกระยาง
nók grà yaang

hornbill
นกเงือก
nók ngêuak

kingfisher
นกกระเต็น
nók grà dten

lark
นกกระจาบฝน
nók grà jàap fŏn

oriole
นกขมิ้น
nók kà mîn

ostrich
นกกระจอกเทศ
nók grà jòrk tâyt

owl
นกฮูก
nók hôok

peacock
นกยูง
nók yoong

pelican
นกกระทุง
nók grà tung

penguin
เพนกวิน
payn gwin

pigeon
นกพิราบ
nók pí râap

sparrow
นกกระจอก
nók grà jòrk

starling
นกกิ้งโครง
nók gîng krohng

stork
นกกระสา
nók grà săa

swan
หงส์
hŏng

thrush
นกเดินดง
nók dern dong

vulture
แร้ง
ráirng

AMPHIBIANS AND REPTILES |
สัตว์ครึ่งบกครึ่งน้ำและสัตว์เลื้อยคลาน

VOCABULARY

tadpole
ลูกอ๊อด
lôok órt

scales
เกล็ด
glèt

to hiss
ทำเสียงขู่
tam sĭang kòo

frogspawn
ไข่กบ
kài gòp

shell
เปลือกหอย
bplèuak hŏy

to croak
ร้องอย่างกบ
rórng yàang gòp

alligator
จระเข้ตีนเป็ด/
แอลลิเกเตอร์
jà rà kây dteen bpèt/airn
lí gay dtêr

frog
กบ
gòp

gecko
ตุ๊กแก
dtúk gair

lizard
จิ้งจก
jîng jòk

newt
นิวต์/กะท่างน้ำ
niw/gà tâang náam

snake
งู
ngoo

toad
คางคก
kaang kók

tortoise
เต่าบก
dtào bòk

turtle
เต่าทะเล
dtào tá lay

234

coral
ปะการัง
bpà gaa rang

crab
ปู
bpoo

dolphin
โลมา
loh maa

eel
ปลาไหล
bplaa lăi

jellyfish
แมงกะพรุน
mairng gà prun

killer whale
วาฬเพชฌฆาต
waan pét chá kâat

lobster
กุ้งล็อบสเตอร์
gûng lóp sà dtêr

seal
แมวน้ำ
maew náam

sea urchin
เม่นทะเล
mên tá lay

shark
ฉลาม
chà lăam

starfish
ดาวทะเล/ปลาดาว
daao tá lay/bplaa daao

whale
วาฬ
waan

VOCABULARY

swarm
ฝูงแมลง
fŏong má lairng

cobweb
ใยแมงมุม/หยากไย่
yai mairng mum/yàak yâi

to buzz
ทำเสียงหึ่งๆ
tam sĭang hèung hèung

colony
อาณาจักร (แมลง)
aa naa jàk (má lairng)

insect bite
แมลงกัด
má lairng gàt

to sting
ต่อย
dtòy

ant
มด
mót

bee
ผึ้ง
pêung

beetle
ด้วง
dûang

butterfly
ผีเสื้อ
pĕe sêua

caterpillar
บุ้ง
bûng

centipede
ตะขาบ
dtà kàap

cockroach
แมลงสาบ
má lairng sàap

cricket
จิ้งหรีด
jîng rèet

dragonfly
แมลงปอ
má lairng bpor

earthworm
ไส้เดือน
sâi deuan

fly
แมลงวัน
má lairng wan

grasshopper
ตั๊กแตน
dták gà dtairn

ladybird
เต่าทอง
dtào torng

mayfly
แมลงชีปะขาว
má lairng chee bpà kǎao

mosquito
ยุง
yung

moth
ผีเสื้อกลางคืน
pěe sêua glaang keuun

slug
ทาก
tâak

snail
หอยทาก
hǒy tâak

spider
แมงมุม
mairng mum

termite
ปลวก
bplùak

wasp
ต่อ
dtòr

VOCABULARY

stalk	pollen	grass
ก้าน	เกสร	หญ้า
gâan	gà săyn	yâa
leaf	bud	seed
ใบ	ยอดอ่อน	เมล็ด
bai	yôrt òrn	zhŏng zi
petal	wildflower	bulb
กลีบ	ดอกไม้ป่า	หัวของพืช
glèep	dòrk máai bpàa	hŭa kŏrng pêuut

YOU SHOULD KNOW...

You may see garlands of flowers known as "puang maa lai". They are used for various spiritual purposes – they may be hung in vehicles to reduce the risk of accidents, or offered to statues in order to pay respect and earn merit.

bougainvillea
เฟื่องฟ้า
fêuang fáa

butterfly pea
อัญชัน
an chan

carnation
คาเนชั่น
kaa nay chân

chrysanthemum
เบญจมาศ
bayn jà màat

frangipani
ลีลาวดี
lee laa wá dee

globe amaranth
บานไม่รู้โรย
baan mâi róo rohy

hibiscus
ชบา
chá baa

ixora
ดอกเข็ม
dòrk kěm

jasmine
มะลิ
má lí

lily
ลิลลี่
lin lêe

lotus
บัว
bua

marigold
ดาวเรือง
daao reuang

orchid
กล้วยไม้
glûay máai

poppy
ป๊อปปี้
bpórp bpêe

rose
กุหลาบ
gù làap

sunflower
ทานตะวัน
taan dtà wan

tulip
ทิวลิป
tiw líp

ylang ylang
กระดังงาไทย
grà dang ngaa tai

VOCABULARY

tree
ต้นไม้
dtôn máai

wood
ไม้
máai

berry
เบอร์รี่
ber rêe

shrub
พุ่ม
pûm

branch
กิ่ง
gìng

root
ราก
râak

orchard
สวนผลไม้
sŭan pŏn lá máai

trunk
ลำต้น
lam dtôn

conifer
ต้นสน
dtôn sŏn

vineyard
ไร่องุ่น
râi à ngùn

bark
เปลือกไม้
bplèuak máai

pine cone/needle
ลูก/ใบสน
lôok/bai sŏn

bodhi tree
ต้นโพธิ์
dtôn poh

camphor tree
ต้นการบูร
dtôn gaan boon

champak
จำปา
jam bpaa

fungus
เห็ด
hèt

golden shower
ราชพฤกษ์
râat chá préuk

grapevine
เถาองุ่น
tăo à ngùn

honeysuckle
สายน้ำผึ้ง
săai nám pêung

Indian almond
หูกวาง
hŏo gwaang

ivy
ไอวี่
ai wêe

lavender
ลาเวนเดอร์
laa wayn der

lichen
ไลเคน
lai kayn

moss
มอส
môrt

pine
ต้นสน
dtôn sŏn

poinciana
หางนกยูง
hăang nók yoong

rain tree
จามจุรี/ฉำฉา
jaam jù ree/chăm chăa

teak
สัก
sàk

Thai crape myrtle
ตะแบกนา
dtà bàirk naa

willow
หลิว
lĭw

VOCABULARY

landscape ทิวทัศน์ tiw tát	estuary ปากแม่น้ำ bpàak mâir náam	rural ชนบท chon ná bòt
soil ดิน din	air อากาศ aa gàat	urban เมือง meuang
mud โคลน klohn	atmosphere บรรยากาศ ban yaa gàat	polar ขั้วโลก kûa lôhk
water น้ำ náam	comet ดาวหาง daao hăang	tropical เขตร้อนชื้น kàyt rórn chéuun

LAND

cave
ถ้ำ
tâm

desert
ทะเลทราย
tá lay saai

farmland
พื้นที่เกษตร
péuun têe gà sàyt

forest
ป่า
bpàa

glacier
ธารน้ำแข็ง
taan nám kěng

grassland
ทุ่งหญ้า
tûng yâa

hill
เนินเขา
nern kǎo

lake
ทะเลสาบ
tá lay sàap

mangrove
ป่าชายเลน
bpàa chaai layn

mountain
ภูเขา
poo kǎo

pond
บึง
beung

river
แม่น้ำ
mâir náam

rocks
ก้อนหิน
gôrn hǐn

scrub
ป่าละเมาะ
bpàa lá mó

stream
ลำธาร
lam taan

valley
หุบเขา
hùp kǎo

volcano
ภูเขาไฟ
poo kǎo fai

waterfall
น้ำตก
nám dtòk

cliff
หน้าผา
nâa păa

coast
ชายฝั่ง
chaai fàng

coral reef
แนวปะการัง
naew bpà gaa rang

island
เกาะ
gò

peninsula
แหลม
lăirm

rockpool
แอ่งน้ำในหิน
èng náam nai hǐn

SKY

aurora
แสงออโรรา/แสงเหนือ
sǎirng or roh râa/sǎirng nĕua

moon
พระจันทร์
prá jan

rainbow
รุ้ง
rúng

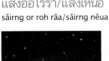

stars
ดาว
daao

sun
พระอาทิตย์
prá aa tít

sunset
พระอาทิตย์ตกดิน
prá aa tít dtòk din

CELEBRATIONS AND FESTIVALS
งานฉลองและเทศกาลรื่นเริง

Celebrations and festivals in Thailand are many and varied. The main event is Songkran, a Thai New Year celebration in April which has become world-famous for its water-splashing customs. Loi Krathong is another big festival in which decorative baskets are floated on the river. Besides these, there are various regional festivals and frequent temple fairs, usually celebrated with lots of food and entertainment.

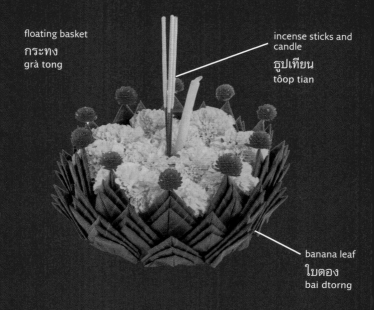

floating basket

กระทง

grà tong

incense sticks and candle

ธูปเทียน

tôop tian

banana leaf

ใบตอง

bai dtorng

YOU MIGHT SAY/HEAR...

Congratulations!
ยินดีด้วย!
yin dee dûay

Best wishes.
ด้วยความปรารถนาดี
dûay kwaam bpràat tà nǎa dee

Well done!
เยี่ยมมาก!
yîam mâak

Thank you.
ขอบคุณ
kòrp kun

Cheers!
ชนแก้ว!
chon gâew

You're very kind.
คุณใจดีมาก
kun jai dee mâak

Happy birthday!
สุขสันต์วันเกิด!
sùk sǎn wan gèrt

Cheers to you, too!
ชนแก้วกัน!
chon gâew gan

Happy anniversary!
สุขสันต์วันครบรอบ!
sùk sǎn wan króp rôrp

Wishing you a prosperous New Year!
สวัสดีปีใหม่ ขอให้ร่ำรวย!
sà wàt dee bpee mài kǒr hâi râm ruay

VOCABULARY

celebration
การฉลอง
gaan chà lǒrng

anniversary
วันครบรอบ
wan króp rôrp

public holiday
วันหยุดราชการ
wan yùt râat chá gaan

birthday
วันเกิด
wan gèrt

wedding anniversary
วันครบรอบแต่งงาน
wan króp rôrp
dtèng ngaan

religious festival
เทศกาลทางศาสนา
tâyt sà gaan taang
sàat sà nǎa

special occasion	bad news	to throw a party
โอกาสพิเศษ	ข่าวร้าย	จัดงานเลี้ยงให้
oh gàat pí sàyt	kàao ráai	jàt ngaan líang hâi

good news	to celebrate	to toast
ข่าวดี	ฉลอง	ขอดื่มให้กับ
kàao dee	chà lŏrng	kŏr dèuum hâi gàp

YOU SHOULD KNOW...

ปลาตะเพียนสาน (bplaa dtà pian săan) is a traditional Thai handicraft modelled on the barb fish and made from plaited and painted palm leaves. They are used as hanging mobiles to be hung over babies' cradles. Since the fish were traditionally regarded as a symbol of abundance and prosperity, the mobiles are seen as auspicious and a way of blessing children with good health and good fortune.

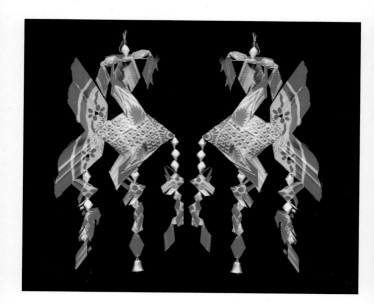

bouquet
ช่อดอกไม้
chôr dòrk máai

box of chocolates
ช็อกโกแลตของขวัญ
chók goh lét kŏrng kwăn

cake
เค้ก
káyk

decorations
ของตกแต่ง
kŏrng dtòk dtèng

fireworks
ดอกไม้ไฟ
dòrk máai fai

fizzy drink
น้ำอัดลม
nám àt lom

greetings card
บัตรอวยพร
bàt uay porn

gift
ของขวัญ
kŏrng kwăn

party
งานเลี้ยง
ngaan líang

VOCABULARY

birth เกิด gèrt	graduation สำเร็จการศึกษา sǎm rèt gaan sèuk sǎa	divorce หย่า yàa
Buddhist ordination การบวช gaan bùat	finding a job ได้งานทำ dâai ngaan tam	having a child มีลูก mee lôok
childhood วัยเด็ก wai dèk	falling in love ตกหลุมรัก dtòk lǔm rák	relocation ย้ายที่อยู่ yáai têe yòo
first day of school ไปโรงเรียนวันแรก bpai rohng rian wan râirk	engagement งานหมั้น ngaan mân	retirement เกษียณอายุ gà sǐan aa yú
passing your driving test สอบได้ใบขับขี่ sòrp dâai bai kàp kèe	marriage แต่งงาน dtèng ngaan	funeral งานศพ ngaan sòp

YOU SHOULD KNOW...

Most Thai Buddhist men are expected to spend some time as a novice monk. The length of ordination varies from person to person.

There are currently 19 annual public holidays in Thailand: these usually relate to festivals, religious observances, and the royal family.

YOU MIGHT SAY/HEAR...

How many days' holiday do we get?
มีวันหยุดกี่วัน
mee wan yùt gèe wan

Is it a holiday today?
วันนี้วันหยุดเหรอ?
wan née wan yùt rěr

What are you celebrating today?
วันนี้คุณฉลองอะไรกัน?
wan née kun chà lŏrng à rai gan

I wish you...
ขออวยพรให้คุณ...
kŏr uay porn hâi kun...

Merry Christmas!
สุขสันต์วันคริสต์มาส!
sùk săn wan krít mâat

Happy New Year!
สวัสดีปีใหม่!
sà wàt dee bpee mài

Happy holidays!
สุขสันต์วันหยุด!
sùk săn wan yùt

And to you, too!
ขอให้คุณมีความสุขด้วย!
kŏr hâi kun mee kwaam sùk dûay

What are your plans for the holiday?
วันหยุดนี้คุณวางแผนทำอะไร
wan yùt née kun waang păirn tam à rai

VOCABULARY

Mother's Day วันแม่ wan mâir	National Day วันชาติ wan châat	New Year's Day วันปีใหม่ wan bpee mài
Father's Day วันพ่อ wan pôr	May Day วันแรงงาน wan rairng ngaan	New Year's card บัตรอวยพรปีใหม่ bàt uay porn bpee mài

| Father Christmas/ Santa Claus ซานตาคลอส saan dtaa klórt | Christmas Day วันคริสต์มาส wan krít mâat | Christmas Eve วันก่อนคริสมาสต์ wan gòrn krít mâat |

If you want to take part in the Loi Krathong festival and float your own basket on the river, make sure you buy a traditional Krathong made from the trunk and leaves of the banana tree (or make your own!).

OTHER FESTIVALS

Children's Day
วันเด็ก
wan dèk

Chinese New Year
วันตรุษจีน
wan dtrùt jeen

Christmas
คริสต์มาส
krít mâat

251

Halloween
ฮัลโลวีน
han loh ween

Loi Krathong Festival
เทศกาลลอยกระทง
tâyt sà gaan loy grà tong

Long Tail Boat Racing Festival
ประเพณีแข่งเรือยาว
bprà pay nee kèng reua yaao

New Year's Eve
คืนปีใหม่
keuun bpee mài

Ramadan
รอมฎอน
ror má dorn

Rocket Festival
บุญบั้งไฟ
bun bâng fai

Thanksgiving
วันขอบคุณพระเจ้า
wan kòrp kun prá jâao

Tomb Sweeping Day
วันเชงเม้ง
wan chayng méng

Valentine's Day
วันวาเลนไทน์
wan waa layn tai

There are various savoury and sweet dishes regarded as auspicious in Thailand and which may be offered in celebration. Egg yolks cooked in syrup are considered to bring luck as they have the word "gold" in the name, while rice noodles are associated with longevity.

FOOD

dumplings
ขนมจีบ
kà nǒm jèep

egg yolks cooked in syrup
ทองหยิบ ทองหยอด
ฝอยทอง
torng yìp torng yòrt fǒy torng

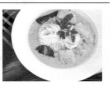

fish curry with rice noodles
ขนมจีนน้ำยา
kà nǒm jeen nám yaa

glass noodles in clear soup
ต้มจืดวุ้นเส้น
dtôm jèuut wún sên

khao chae (soaked rice)
ข้าวแช่
kâao châir

layered coconut dessert
ขนมชั้น
kà nǒm chán

mango and sticky rice
ข้าวเหนียวมะม่วง
kâao nǐaw má mûang

pad Thai
ผัดไทย
pàt tai

spicy minced meat salad
ลาบ
lâap

steamed fish curry in
banana leaf
ห่อหมก
hòr mòk

steamed muffin
ขนมถ้วยฟู
kà nǒm tûay foo

whole fish
ปลาทั้งตัว
bplaa táng dtua

DRINKS

butterfly pea and lime
drink
น้ำอัญชันมะนาว
nám an chan má naao

lemongrass drink
น้ำตะไคร้
nám dtà krái

longan drink
น้ำลำไย
nám lam yai

YOU SHOULD KNOW...

Common alcoholic drinks in Thailand include beer and wine coolers. Various brands of rum (referred to locally as "whiskey"), typically mixed with ice and soda water, are also a popular choice. The sale of alcohol is banned during certain religious holidays.

In addition to Songkran, there are various Buddhist festivals throughout the year, such as Asanha Bucha, which involves a candlelight procession around a temple in a clockwise direction. This is followed by the beginning of Buddhist Lent. Traditional activities during these festivals include building sand pagodas to honour Buddha, and giving jasmine garlands as gifts or placing them at shrines.

YOU MIGHT SAY/HEAR...

Happy Songkran!
สุขสันต์วันสงกรานต์
sùk sǎn wan sǒng graan

Are you going home for Songkran this year?
ปีนี้กลับบ้านวันสงกรานต์ไหม
bpee née glàp bâan wan sǒng graan mái

What day is New Year this year?
ปีใหม่ปีนี้วันอะไร
bpee mài bpee née wan à rai

Would you like to join my family for New Year celebrations?
คุณอยากมาฉลองปีใหม่กับครอบครัวของ ผม/ฉัน ไหม
kun yàak maa chà lǒrng bpee mài gàp krôrp krua kǒrng pǒm/chán mái

I have a small gift for you.
ผม/ฉัน มีของขวัญเล็กๆ น้อยๆ ให้คุณ
pǒm/chán mee kǒrng kwǎn lék lék nóy nóy hâi kun

Please come and eat with us.
มาทานข้าวกับพวกเราเถอะ ครับ/ค่ะ
maa taan kâao gàp pûak rao tùh kráp/kâ

candlelight procession
เวียนเทียน
wian tian

jasmine garland
พวงมาลัยดอกมะลิ
puang maa lai dòrk má lí

making a sand pagoda
ก่อเจดีย์ทราย
gòr jay dee saai

marlstone
ดินสอพอง
din sŏr porng

National Elderly Day
วันผู้สูงอายุแห่งชาติ
wan pôo sŏong aa yú
hèng châat

offering alms to monks
ทำบุญตักบาตร
tam bun dtàk bàat

pouring water on a
statue of Buddha
สรงน้ำพระ
sŏng náam prá

pouring water on older
people's hands
รดน้ำดำหัวผู้ใหญ่
rót náam dam hŭa pôo yài

scented water
น้ำอบ
nám òp

Songkran festival parade
ประกวดเทพีสงกรานต์
bprà gùat tay pee
sŏng graan

Songkran migration
กลับบ้านวันสงกรานต์
glàp bâan wan sŏng graan

water fun
เล่นน้ำสงกรานต์
lên náam sŏng graan

YOU SHOULD KNOW...

Songkran is the biggest festival in Thailand and is the Thai New Year
celebration, in accordance with the Buddhist calendar. One of the associated
traditions is pouring water onto Buddha statues, and onto the hands of young
or elderly people. This has evolved into large-scale water fights in the streets –
a popular way to cool down during the hottest part of the year.

259

263

PHOTO CREDITS

Shutterstock: p21 timetable (Brendan Howard), p26 red car (JazzBoo), p29 ticket machine (Balakate), p29 traffic police (Ida Jelly), p32 checkpoint (SARIN KUNTHONG), p32 tyre pump (Cattleya2017), p34 minibus (Iakov Filimonov), p40 BTS Skytrain (Worchi Zingkhai), p40 couchette (moxumbic), p40 locomotive (edusma7256), p41 network map (Sittirak Jadlit), p41 ticket machine (Balakate), p41 ticket office (Kevin Hellon), p82 marketplace (2p2play), p104 confectionery (Bitkiz), p107 accessories (StockCo), p107 cosmetics (mandritoiu), p107 food and drink (1000 words), p107 footwear (Toshio Chan), p107 kitchenware (NikomMaelao Production), p107 toys (Zety Akhzar), p115 electrical retailer (BestPhotoPlus), p115 estate agency (Barry Barnes), p116 gift shop (Pamela Loreto Perez), p116 pet shop (BestPhotoPlus), p137 campus (EQRoy), p142 bureau de change (Lloyd Carr), p144 postbox (Wanz.st), p144 stamp (tulpahn), p145 church (Ilya Images), p145 conference centre (lou armor), p146 police station (Phuong D. Nguyen), p146 retail park (Sumeth anu), p146 town hall (Suptar), p151 audio guide (Aleksandra Suzi), p151 museum (thebigland), p151 sightseeing bus (Cooler8), p151 tour guide (Kittipong Chararoj), p153 cabaret show (Yasemin Yurtman Candemir), p154 coffee house (amabird), p154 musical (Igor Bulgarin), p154 night market (BREEZY STOCK), p154 opera (criben), p164 temple fair (NS.photographer), p166 choir (Marco Saroldi), p166 orchestra (Ferenc Szelepcsenyi), p175 scoreboard (feelphoto), p180 football pitch (Christian Bertrand), p183 line judge (Leonard Zhukovsky), p183 umpire (Stuart Slavicky), p184 basketball shoes (Milos Vucicevic), p192 velodrome (Pavel L Photo and Video), p194 sepak takraw (Mohd Nasirruddin Yazid), p218 labour suite (ChameleonsEye), p243 YOU SHOULD KNOW… image (adul24), p251 Children's Day (Igor Bulgarin), p252 Long Tail Boat Racing Festival (SIHASAKPRACHUM), p252 Rocket Festival (yaipearn), p252 Tomb Sweeping Day (Arnon Mungyodklang), p255 candlelight procession (Ggamies), p256 offering alms to monks (chin797), p256 Songkran festival parade (Valoga), p256 Songkran migration (Ninja Artist). All other images from Shutterstock.